Golden Years
of
Walsall

The publishers would like to thank the following companies for their

support in the production of this book

Main Sponsor

Caldmore Area Housing Association Limited

AAC Limited

Aldridge Plastics

Ancol Pet Products Limited

Birchill Automotive Presswork Limited

Bullock Bros

Albert Jagger Limited

Modern Saddlery (Walsall) / Gabriel Power & Co

William Price and Sons Limited

First published in Great Britain by True North Books Limited

England HX3 6AE

01422 344344

ISBN 1 903204 56 9

Text, design and origination by True North Books Limited

Printed and bound by The Amadeus Press Limited

Golden Years
of
Walsall

Contents

Introduction

In quiet moments we all sit back to reflect on the past. We dream of those days of yesteryear when everything seemed so much sunnier, when we were more content with life as it was. Perhaps we are fooling ourselves, but it is no sin to draw comfort from experiences through which we have lived or about which our parents told us. It does help to have a prop to help and that is where 'Golden Years of Walsall' will play its part. Within these pages is a wealth of nostalgia spanning the middle years of the last century. As the reader leafs through the book many half forgotten memories will come flooding back. Things that an older generation told us of will be there in black and white, firming up the mental images of a Walsall that seemed to be locked into a time capsule out of our reach. The lovely photographs and accompanying text, variously informative, poignant and wry, help bring back to life a town that has changed so much as the years have unfolded. It is not just the buildings, skylines and thoroughfares that have altered but

a whole way of life. The pace of the days when we were young or our parents were alive is brought back to life within this nostalgic trip down memory lane. With the turning of each page will come a visit to Bridge Street when the Walsall Mutual Building Society looked after our money and we danced at the Mayfair Ballroom, a stroll along High Street as the 'beaks' dispensed justice from the magistrates' court in the Guildhall and a stopover at one of the many pubs that flourished close to Church Hill.

But it is not only the sights of the town that have changed. Even the vocabulary of the era that we examine in 'Golden Years of Walsall' has undergone a transformation. Then we spent tanners, bobs and half crowns as we did our shopping. Everything was weighed out on scales that measured in pounds and ounces without fear of shopkeepers being prosecuted by our lords and masters in government who seem to regard metrication as a god to be worshipped. We ran up curtains by the inch, not the centimetre, and used words like 'please' and 'thank you'.

An aerial view of Walsall in the mid 20th century.

'Good morning' was a phrase used as we passed someone in the street without fear of being accused of harassment. Our children called neighbours 'uncle' or 'aunty', but now they are not spoken to because we do not even know their names. Mugging meant looking at someone's face, crack was a joke or a gap in the pavement and joyriding was a happy journey. Now we have spin in politics when once it was the prerogative of Eric Hollies, Jim Laker or Hedley Verity. But, with every hankering for the return of the old times and their values there must be some realism that it was not all days of wine and roses. There were also slum properties, areas of poverty and deprivation and the sheer horror of a world war that brought death and destruction raining down from the skies as enemy planes bombed our factories and homes.

Walsall has a long history and, we are sure, a vibrant future. It is up to our next generations to create that future, but they will be helped by drawing on the experiences and lessons learned from the past. First recorded mention of our town was made in the early years of the last millennium. A will from this time, dated 1002, makes reference to 'Walesho', possibly meaning 'home of the woods'. However, there are many other similar name forms that make reference to this location in the early 11th century, including 'Wealhs Halh', which is probably an old English form of language meaning land or shelter belonging to Wealh. There is various speculation that Wealh was the personal name of a chieftain, but it may also have simply meant 'Briton' or 'Welshman'. Surprisingly, no mention of any spelling of Walsall is recorded in the 1086 Domesday Book that was compiled on the orders of William the Conqueror. Whether this was an oversight or a dirty trick played by a future 'Baggies' supporter is unknown.

What is certain is that in the Middle Ages the town grew in a cross shape around Church Hill, the town's highest point at 511 feet. Formerly dedicated as All Saints, a church has stood on this spot since the early 13th century. Now St Matthew's, it still displays evidence of its illustrious past in its Norman arch and original inner crypt. The old town stretched to Town End and along Rushall Street and Peal Street. The modern market on High Street can rightly claim an 800 year ancestry having first been mentioned c1220. Walsall developed as an important agricultural centre and market town, but there were early hints of its later claim to fame when light metalworking began to have

A bustling High Street Market in March 1965.

some influence in Tudor times. Buckles, bits, stirrups and spurs were forerunners of the trade that would put Walsall on the international map during the Victorian era. As with many other midland and northern towns the Industrial Revolution thrust Walsall into prominence. Good stocks of coal, iron and limestone were mined locally and the little industries became major concerns. Excellent canal links and, by the middle of the 19th century, a railway network enabled easy movement of heavy goods. The population of the town exploded from its 10,000 in 1800 to a figure several times greater by the end of the century. By then the high concentration on leather goods and saddlery had turned Walsall from being just another little town in central England to one that was known across the world as the Leather Capital of Britain. Changes to the old town were wrought at the beginning of the last century when many of the old buildings around Church Hill were demolished. This had been a crowded and insanitary area, made all the more uninspiring by the slum nature of the housing and proliferation of drinking dens to be found. In keeping with national patterns there was much redevelopment in the town during the 1960s. Many fine old buildings were lost as they fell into disrepair or were simply demolished to make way for new town centre refurbishment and road remodelling. At least 'Golden Years of Walsall' will help the reader rediscover some of the proud architecture that was surrendered to the planners' whims and the demolition men's cranes.

Now there is an opportunity to return to a time when we put silver joeys inside Christmas puddings and sucked on Spangles and gobstoppers. Sing along to Dickie Valentine on that scratchy 78 or chuckle at the exploits of Laurel and Hardy in the 'Film Fun' comic. Put gravy browning on your legs because nylon stockings are not available and tune in to Henry Hall's orchestra on radio's Light Programme. Perm your hair with a Toni or wear it held back by an Alice band. Reach for a Craven A cigarette, 'for your throat's sake' as the adverts told us, and stand up as the headmaster enters the classroom. It is time to turn to the next page and begin a voyage into nostalgia aboard your very own Tardis, whisked off to a time when dad tipped up his pay packet for mum to put into jars labelled 'rent', 'housekeeping', 'milkman', 'insurance' and 'coal'. The golden years' time machine is about to leave.

Street scenes

Dudley Street is unrecognisable now as the place where this photograph was taken of brightly coloured material and union flags fluttering in the breeze. The exact date is not known but the bunting might well have been flown as part of the celebrations for the coronation of George VI or his father's 1935 silver jubilee. The White Swan and the Duke of York were two of Walsall's oldest pubs. The latter, at 31 Dudley Street, with premises next door occupied by a chimney sweep, was a wattle and daub, timber framed building dating from Tudor times. The old walling was exposed prior to its closure on 10 August 1937. The name and licence were transferred to other premises on Lumley Road where the landlord and drinkers could enjoy lavatories, a bathroom and flushing facilities not present in the old Duke of York. Dudley Street, once called Hole End, is one of the town's oldest streets, leading off to Wednesbury and Dudley. It was crammed with small houses that backed into the hillside. Many lacked a back door or yard and residents had to fetch water from a standpipe further down the street, not far from the communal privy. Not everybody can look back nostalgically on the good old days. The demolition of all this property did not come a moment too soon.

The animals went in two by two, for to get out of the rain. So did the cars on Sunday, 14 June 1931 for this was one of the many occasions when Walsall was flooded. Here a torrential downpour had dumped two inches of rain on the town in just 45 minutes. The drivers inched their way carefully towards a higher level, anxious not to get damp on their spark plugs and carburettor points. Children were keener on the rain than their parents. They jumped in and out of the flow, splashing away merrily until being on the wrong end of a severe ticking off for being a nuisance. The installation of a storm drain along Park Street later in the 1930s helped alleviate the problems that the weather had often brought, but until then such sights were commonplace here and around the station whenever the heavens opened. The poor shopkeepers must have despaired when they saw their stock being ruined by the floodwaters rushing into their cellars and shop floors. It was not only the damage caused there and then but also the mud and debris left behind that took so long to clear when the waters receded. There was also that foetid smell that lingered for ages. This watery power of mother nature is something we still have not tamed. Even in the 21st century there are homes and businesses that cannot get insurance because they are sited in a high risk flood area.

Left: Rushall Street is cut in two where it meets Ablewell Street. The latter road takes its name from Aval Walle, old French that means 'below the fortified wall'. Here we are looking north into Lower Rushall Street, part of the old road that led to the once thriving village built on the 'marsh land where rushes grow' that has lost its individuality to housing developments and road improvements. Rushall was once a spot where the hoi polloi lived and, behind the camera, Upper Rushall Street had a former claim to be one of Walsall's main streets. The road is much busier today, with traffic heading towards the A461 to Lichfield, than it was in 1936. Then, motoring was a more sedate affair. Pedestrians could stroll across the street with relative ease, though it must be said that road safety was a major issue in those days. The number of accidents and casualties were out of all proportion to the

volume of traffic, leading to a number of precautionary measures such as pedestrian crossings, electrically controlled traffic lights, cats' eyes and driving tests being introduced on a large scale during this decade. The fashion of the women on the left typified the style of the time, all tight waists and full length skirts. A few years later they would be exchanged for shorter, utility dresses as clothing rationing was introduced.

Below: According to the poster the London Midland and Scottish railway was the best way to travel. It probably was until nationalisation came along after the war and the big companies were rolled together into one as the Labour government brought them under state control. Camp coffee, being advertised on another hoarding, is that quaint blend of sugar, water, coffee and chicory that has somehow managed to survive down the years. To some it has a consistency not dissimilar to engine sump oil. But, it has its fans, just as it did in 1930. The people trudging along the cobbled Walsall Street in Willenhall could not have related to the picture on the bottle of the Highland soldier and his Indian attendant, but at least a cup of the stuff might warm them up. Willenhall developed from being an agricultural village into a thriving mining community until the mines were flooded in the 19th century and ceased production. Lockmaking then became its main industry and that bred its own unique problems. Many men spent so long hunched over their workbenches that they developed spinal deformities. Willenhall was then cruelly nicknamed 'Humpshire'. It became part of Walsall Borough in 1966, but still boasts its own identity and that is helped by having the M6 motorway as a form of eastern border.

Bottom: The car turning the corner was retracing the steps of the hooves of noble steeds from more than a century before. Bouncing along the bottom end of New Street, heading north, was something of a bone shaking ride in 1936, but it had been even more so in earlier times as this was the former main coach road to Birmingham. Teams of horses pulling passenger laden vehicles or mail coaches pounded the stage routes in the 18th and 19th centuries before the age of steam brought the railway network that revolutionised public transport and the movement of goods around the country. In April 1771 the Wolverhampton, Willenhall, Walsall and Birmingham stage began a weekly service that opened up parts of the Midlands that locals had never previously visited. Turnpikes, with their toll booths that generated the cash for the upkeep of the roads, provided a previously static population with the opportunity to spread its wings, though it was the locomotive that was to encourage people to be more mobile. New Street was once Newgate Street, created to provide another route to and from the cramped development near St Matthew's and Church Hill. There were six yards of 50 houses tucked away behind the front dwellings, not to mention a large number of drinking houses that seemed so out of place close to a place of worship.

Left: Whoever these little boys were and however respectful to adults they usually might have been we do not need much imagination to put words into their mouths if they were making comparisons about the two main subjects of this picture. Had they been overheard a clip around the ear would have been their just desserts and no one would have blamed the woman for giving them just that. Nor would the lads have complained to their parents. If they found out another smack would have been the result. There was a time when parents accepted that teachers, police and other adults were within their rights to dish out a spot of corporal punishment. How often have you heard a parent say today 'Well, it never did me any harm' and then rush off to pound the headteacher's door because someone has had the brass neck to say 'boo' to little Kylie. This scene was being played out at Ryecroft, an area formerly famous for the fine sand for glassmaking and the loam used in neighbouring iron foundries. In the 18th century Ryecroft Farm covered 200 acres. Later, one area near Ryecroft Street became so run down that it became known as Pigsty Park, but perhaps the porker in the picture knew that.

Below: The photographer was just in time to capture this view of a court on the southeast side of the bottom part of Lower Rushall Street in 1937. Not long after the image was recorded for posterity demolition of these properties was under way. The living conditions were poor as there was little in the way of modern amenities or decent sanitation. Crowded on top of each other the houses provided a breeding ground for disease and offered a life that was little more than mere existence level. Despite that they had something that is lacking in today's society. There was a real sense of community in these courts. People pulled together, helping one another out. Those who fell on hard times could rely on a helping hand from a neighbour, even one whose straits were almost as dire. Hippies who went to live in communes in the 60s and 70s thought that they had invented a life where possessions and responsibilities were shared, but they merely built on the example of such communities as this one. The pooling of resources may have been less formalised, but it was just as real. You would not see your neighbour go short nor a child go hungry. The courts were also a great place to hone soccer skills. With a couple of dustbins for goalposts and a moth-eaten tennis ball being bounced off walls and along cobbles a lad could spend many happy hours mastering the art that might just make him another Stanley Matthews or Tom Finney.

arlaston was part of the 19th century population explosion. It increased four fold during that century to reach over 15,000. In the workshops the manufacture of gun locks, nuts and bolts were particularly important. However, improvements to housing conditions did not keep the same pace and it was a depressing place until a great deal of new housing swept away the slums in the 1950s. King Street, seen here in 1950, had some of Darlaston's finest houses in medieval times. It progressed to become the premier shopping area. It was pedestrianised as King Street Precinct in the 1970s. The roundabout marks a spot where the barbaric pastime of bull baiting used to occur. Still known as Bull Stake poor creatures were tethered here to await their grisly fate. Before we get too sanctimonious and

condemn our forefathers let us firstly look across Europe and take in a bull fight in Spain. Then we can turn our gaze homewards to those in red coats sitting astride horses and blowing little horns as they hunt down Mr Reynard. Perhaps we have not become quite as civilised as we thought we had. Even so, it must have been a horrid experience for a frightened bull to undergo such a dreadful experience as crowds bayed,

quite literally, for its blood. Tied by a leg or its neck to a stake its nose was often blown full of pepper to further arouse it. Specially trained dogs were loosed singly, each attempting to seize the tethered animal's nose. Often, a hole in the ground was provided for the bull to protect its snout. A successful dog was said to have pinned the bull. The practice was only finally outlawed in 1835.

In 1960 the Guildhall on High Street was not marooned from the rest of the town centre as it is today. Its foundation stone was laid on 24 July 1865 and still served as the borough's police and magistrates' court until 1976. It replaced a former Guildhall that had been there since the beginning of the 19th century. One of the earlier buildings bearing the same title became the town hall during the 16th century, though the Green Dragon Inn took up part of it. The whole edifice was given a makeover in 1986 when the Guildhall was turned into shops and offices that now include an Italian restaurant. The Green Dragon was relicensed at the same time. Guild halls were originally places where associations of craftsmen or merchants met. These groups were formed for mutual aid and protection and for the furtherance of their professional interests. The guilds were thus able to pass legislative measures regulating all economic activity in the town. Gradually this evolved into the wider social control given to local politicians and officers that we now know. At the time of this view of High Street we were enjoying boom years the like of which we had never seen before. Even the prime minister, Harold Macmillan, had been moved to say that we had never had it so good as the Tories retained power in the general election a few months earlier. As the 60s began Michael Holliday was on top of the hit parade with 'Starry Eyed' and it was an apt comment on how we were all feeling.

used standard vehicles for many years. Patrolmen, kitted out with a uniform and huge gauntlets, travelled the highways preparing to lend roadside assistance to any member whose car had broken down. Cars were nowhere near as reliable as they are today and on a trip to the seaside it was commonplace to see vehicles on the verges, bonnets up and radiators boiling over. If a patrolman saw a car heading towards him that displayed a member's badge the driver would receive a smart salute.

Above: The majority of the cars on High Street in 1961 still bore the hallmark of British manufacture. The invasion by Toyota, Nissan, Datsun and the others was yet to materialise. There was something rather reassuring about the names of the models that we once drove. Hillman Imp, Riley Elf, Morris Cowley, Vauxhall Victor and Austin Cambridge were so quintessentially British, unlike the exotic titles bestowed on cars in the modern era. Motoring has seen major developments over the last 50 years that has meant that sacrificing traditional names is but a small price to pay. Who can forget trying to crank an engine into life with a starting handle on a cold and frosty morning in the 1950s? Unreliable or nonexistent heaters and frozen rear windows are hardly nostalgic features that we would welcome back. What would we have given back then for a car whose subframe did not rust away beneath our feet, making us roll up our trouser legs as we drove in the rain? But there are some other things on High Street whose passing we really can mourn. The George Hotel on the left was pulled down in 1979 and has disappeared without a trace and is becoming a fast receding memory. It has been replaced by a modern brick building that can never hope to rival the majesty and glory of its predecessor.

Left: This is the Portobello High Street, Willenhall before the dual carriageway was built. Brickmaking was once an important industry in this area and, as with other industries, a small community grew up around the main source of employment. The motorcycle and sidecar cuts a lonely figure and is one seldom seen today. In the middle years of the last century it was a popular mode of transport. A small family that was unable to afford a car found this an alternative means of getting around. It was cheaper to buy and more economical to run. A sidecar did not have such a good safety record because the passenger in the cab was very vulnerable in the event of a road accident. However, the racing model of these vehicles provided exciting sport on the racetrack as the passenger alternately leant across the back of the machine or sideways across the tarmac to give greater stability. The AA and RAC

Below: Wimpey was one of the large building contractors that built the houses on the housing estates that sprang up after the war when local and national governments pushed hard to replenish the country's housing stocks. Redevelopment was shelved for obvious reasons during the war and there were other priorities in the immediate postwar recovery days. Bombing had destroyed so many homes and by the 1950s the problems were becoming so acute that all the stops were pulled out to improve our living standards. There was also a shift in public attitude towards home ownership. In the early 20th century most people lived in rented accommodation. Buying your own house was not regarded as an important status symbol. As people began to appreciate that inflation was pushing up house prices they realised the value of investing in bricks and mortar. Brownhills was no exception to the housing boom, hence the Wimpey hoarding on Anchor Bridge, High Street on 25 September 1961. A toll house once operated near this spot, charging travellers on the road varying amounts dependent upon the type of vehicle they drove or the number of livestock they were herding. The town probably took its name from the spoil and slag heaps created by the coal mines. In 1858 a railway line was cut through the middle of the early mining settlement and the community moved east towards High Street. Coal mining was still an important industry into the 1950s. Brownhills became part of Walsall MBC in 1974.

Right: The traffic at a standstill on Bridge Street on 7 November 1967 shows how badly congested town and city centres were becoming as car ownership boomed. One way systems, bus only lanes, park and ride, pedestrianisation, swingeing parking fees and tolls have all been tried to help give the centres back to the people, but no one has solved the problem, merely moving it somewhere else. The vehicles had halted outside Tudor House, a grand building that still has a splendour as it graces this part of Walsall today. Designed by HE Lavender and completed in 1926, it has delightfully carved Tudor roses on its downspouts and facade. The entrance to the old Observer offices is at the far end of the building. The top floors are now upmarket flats and apartments and individual commercial units that include an amusement arcade, building society, chemist and estate agent occupy the ground floor. Cinemagoers once went in droves to the Odeon, to the right of Tudor House. It started life as the Picture House, a luxurious cinema with an oak panelled foyer and lifts to the balcony that opened on 29 July 1920. An orchestra played music by Wagner and Strauss to add to the feeling of opulence. It became the Gaumont in 1948 and changed to the Odeon in 1965. Destroyed by fire in 1971, it lay derelict for years and the site is now part of Tesco's.

Above: Cars no longer bowl along the now pedestrianised Park Street as they did in 1969. The centrepiece of this photograph is an excellent reminder of the care that architects and builders took in creating their buildings before utility became the watchword. When the Red Lion was rebuilt in 1896 every effort was made to give it some character. Figurines, carvings and neatly rounded domes, all topped off by the noble king of the jungle, gave locals so much to look at and admire. The uniform, oblong lines of the building to the right is in stark contrast and is just the sort of structure that could be deposited anywhere for it has no soul of its own to mark it out from the rest. The Red Lion is part of the alcoholic history of Britain. There was a pecking order about the hostelries on our streets. Inns were places where accommodation and refreshment could be obtained, taverns sold wine and ale and beerhouses were exactly what they said they were. At the top of the town, around Church Hill, there used to be a host of popular drinking places. The church was not averse to their presence as drinking parties, even back in Puritan times, provided useful supplementary income.

Top right: In 1960 we entered the decade that will be forever known as the swinging 60s, or at least it will until 2060 comes along. It was to be a period when the youth of this country demanded and received attention. Young people had both money and bras to burn as they became a powerhouse in the market place and in the shaping of political and social ideals. They brought a freshness and a brashness to music and fashion, kicking out the conformity of their parents and replacing it with individuality. Women's hemlines shot up as men's hair lengths came down. Protest was in the air as the status quo was challenged and flower stems thrust into gun barrels. Dance bands contracted into beat groups and women

started to go into pubs on their own without the need of a male chaperon. As the decade opened the Talbot Hotel and High Street were not quite ready for such a transformation, steeped as they still were in the culture of those first postwar years. The Talbot, once known as Sherwin's, was a long established hostelry with links to the Talbot family, who, as the Earls of Shrewsbury, were prominent in the Hundred Years' War and in royal circles in Hanoverian times. During World War I, when drunkenness was regarded by Lloyd George as an enemy second only to Germany, the clerk to the justices told the Talbot's licensee his 'premises were ill conducted'. However they were run they did not swing long into the 60s, closing down in January 1963.

Far right: Before the New Road was built Wolverhampton Street was the main route leading out to the west of town. At one time stagecoaches clattered along this road, but in 1969 the horseless carriage had long been king. However, it was a monarch that was becoming increasingly difficult to control. Double yellow lines, parking meters and no waiting signs started to appear everywhere in an attempt to improve traffic flow on our increasingly congested streets. The measures seem

to have succeeded here to the extent that there is hardly a moving vehicle in sight. Car ownership had really taken off during this decade, no longer being the privilege of the middle classes. What had once been a luxury item became one of life's necessities. The oil companies competed greedily with one another for a motorist's business. In addition to using traditional hoardings, as Texaco did, television adverts became increasingly important as this medium was now a fixture in virtually every household. 'Keep going well, keep going Shell' and Esso's 'put a tiger in your tank' were just two examples of catchy slogans used to seduce us into using these companies' filling stations. Even our vocabulary changed because we used to top up our tanks at garages.

Events & occasions

There was not a square inch of space free outside the town hall on 6 October 1927 when a civic welcome to rival any ever witnessed before or since was afforded to Flight Lieutenant Webster. He was no pop star or conquering hero, but his exploits were féted nevertheless. This aviator was part of the Supermarine team, based in Southampton, that competed successfully in the Schneider Trophy race. Supermarine's S for Schneider series of seaplanes were sleek, fast monoplanes developed as twin float racers in the 1920s with the express aim of setting records and winning trophies. It was a happy mix of the cavalier and the commitment to development of a young and thrusting industry that tested and adapted under competitive conditions. Webster's S5 was capable of speeds approaching 250 mph. This was a fantastic achievement considering that it was less than 25 years since the Wright brothers made the first powered flight at Kitty Hawk. The public was captivated by swift developments and the pioneering pilots became household names. Louis Blériot flew the Channel in 1909, Alcock and Brown crossed the Atlantic in 1919 and Charles Lindbergh crossed the same ocean alone in 1927. Women would make their mark in this field as well. Amelia Earhart matched Lindbergh's achievement in 1932 and England's Amy Johnson astounded the world with her flights to Australia, South Africa and across Siberia in the 1930s.

In 1859 Walsall became only the third town in Britain to open its own library. The present one on Lichfield Street opened in 1906 thanks largely to a donation by the philanthropist Andrew Carnegie. Next to it stands the memorial statue to John Henry Carless, that brave young man who lost his life in the service of his country at Heligoland Bight on 17 November 1917. Carless was born in 1896. There is a sad irony in the actual date of his birth for it fell on 11 November, nowadays marked as Remembrance Day when we give thanks each year for all those who fell during two world wars. John Carless was rejected for army service when he failed a medical, but joined the Royal Navy in September 1913. Whilst serving on HMS Caledon as a gun rammer the ship came under enemy fire. Despite being severely wounded he stayed at his post helping clear away other casualties and cheering on the replacement crew. Eventually he collapsed and died from his injuries, but his actions had inspired the spirits of everyone around him. Six months later it was announced that he had been awarded the Victoria Cross. Peace was declared on what would have been his 22nd birthday. The monument was unveiled on 21 February 1920 and, three years later, Oxford Street, Caldmore was renamed Carless Street in his honour. Here Lord Jellicoe, admiral of the British fleet at the Battle of Jutland, paid his respects by laying a wreath at a memorial service on 12 October 1930.

J olly times and jolly rogers came together as part of the enjoyment that went with the 1930 Walsall hospitals' carnival and féte. Pirates swashed their buckle and condemned others to walk the plank aboard this fine float that was one of many to delight the huge crowds that thronged the pavements. They lined the route as local bands played, scouts and guides marched and nurses encouraged everyone to open their purses and empty their wallets in such a good cause. Walsall folk responded positively, even if times were hard and jobs scarce in those depression years. The carnival proces-

sion and the fun of the fair afterwards gave some respite from the worries of juggling family finances. Little children ran in and out of the gaps between the floats, playing a sort of 'chicken' game before being brought firmly back to heel by their parents. Notice that there was hardly a bare head to be seen amongst the spectators. It was part of accepted fashion that men wore caps or hats. Women pulled on bonnets or donned hats that varied between the older cloche style and the new wider brimmed look. Whatever your class or station in life it was not the done thing to go onto the streets bare headed.

Below: Every ball has its belle and every carnival its queen. The prized crown of the 1930 Walsall hospitals' carnival would be proudly worn for a whole year until it was time to choose a successor. It was an auspicious moment for this elegant recipient and she gathered all her poise and elegance about her as the symbol of her reign was carefully lowered onto her neatly coiffured head. Her attendants shared the moment with a mixture of pleasure and envy, for in truth they would have given their eye-teeth to be in her place. The look on their faces did not give the game away, but it would not be too unkind to suggest that one or two of those smiles masked gritted teeth. The younger pair of girls thought of the day in the future when their turn might come around. If ever it did let us hope that they carried their crowns with the same charm and dignity as the 1930 queen displayed. There was no punching the air in celebration, no whoop of delight. This young lady carried the day in a manner that befitted such an honour and the only emotion shown was spotted when a tear of pride trickled down her mother's cheek as she watched the ceremony from the body of the crowd opposite.

Right: The coronation of George VI in 1937 was the inspiration behind joyous celebrations up and down the country. It was a time to push the boat out, or in this case the float. His subjects did not know their new king well. They did not have television programmes that brought his image into the living room as happens to royalty today. The occasional newspaper photograph or item on a cinema newsreel was about the only chance to catch a glimpse of him until the abdication crisis forced him into the limelight. Albert, Duke of York had been happy to play second fiddle to his more charismatic brother. It was a shock to his system when he realised that he was going to have to accept a crown that he hoped would not turn into a poisoned chalice. A nervous, shy man with a pronounced stutter, George VI was fortunate to be married to Elizabeth Bowes-Lyon. She would guide and support him throughout his reign with that winning smile on her face that won so many hearts. The message on this coronation display, 'Long may they reign', was an unfulfilled prophecy. King George died less than 15 years after his coronation, but in that time he had managed to restore a faith in the monarchy that his brother had sorely tested. His queen survived him by 50 years, being forever remembered as the glorious and sadly missed Queen Mum.

Below: It was a proud day for the country when King George VI was crowned. Veterans of the first world war were given pride of place on the front row as they listened to the speeches that heralded the celebrations that took place here and all over the country. Royal standards and union flags were unfurled and bunting flew everywhere. As well as a sense of pride in our monarchy there was also an overriding feeling of relief that the great day had at last arrived and now the nation could settle into a period of stability again. It had been a difficult time. When George V died in January 1936 the smooth succession by his eldest son was but a formality. As Prince of Wales Edward had been groomed for the position for many years. However, his popularity with the public came to be sorely tested when news of his long running affair with the twice divorced American socialite Wallis Simpson became widely known and a subject of heated debate that divided the nation. His decision to marry her cost him the throne and he abdicated in December. His brother took his place and the coronation date of 12 May 1937, pencilled in for Edward VIII, was filled by George VI.

The 1933 carnival procession had reached Bridge Street and there just seemed to be no end to the parade of bands, floats and marching groups that entertained the large crowd that had turned out. It was a good opportunity for some proud parents to admire the musicianship of their offspring playing in the junior bands. Others had spent hours sewing costumes for their children to wear so that they could take their places on the floats, dressed as characters in some imaginative tableau. As a nation we had often taken to the streets in the first third of the last century. During the Great War we waved off the troops as they marched to war and cheered them as they returned four years later. In the 1920s people were out in force

protesting at wage cuts and longer hours in the workplace, conditions that provoked a general strike in 1926. But the carnival was a procession in which we could participate happily. Great pleasure was derived from such simple events and how we loved to strut our stuff in the last century. As well as the carnival we had the Whit walks when church groups paraded around the streets and little ones got new clothes that were put away afterwards for use on high days and holidays. After walking behind a banner the youngsters went off to visit an old aunty or uncle they had not seen for ages, hopeful of a small addition to their piggy banks. 'Must be Whitsun, then', muttered one grumpy relative as he answered the door being pounded by an eager little tot.

Above: The Air Raid Precautions (ARP) service was started before World War II began. The country had at last woken up to the threat of Fascism that had dominated Germany and Italy and had reared its head in Spain during the civil war in that country (1936-39). The threat to civilians that enemy aircraft posed was brought graphically home when the Basque town of Guernica was virtually wiped off the map in 1937. At home civil defence groups started to practise emergency evacuation movements, gas mask drills and rescue procedures. Unfortunately, despite the evidence of their eyes and ears, reaction from the masses was slow. They were also lulled into a false sense of security by Prime Minister Chamberlain's assurance that he had secured peace in our time on his visit to Munich in 1938. One week after he returned the Germans marched into Czechoslovakia. The threat of war was now very real and the defence of our homeland became a reality when the balloon finally went up. How grateful we became for those brave men and women who went on fire watch and blackout duties. They supported the fire and ambulance services as the bombs were falling, putting their own lives at risk for the greater benefit of us all. The ARP was important to Walsall as the town was only eight miles from Birmingham and also had its own marshalling yard and railway junction at Bescot. Walsall and District Co-operative Society presented this ARP van to the service.

The parade of Queen Mary's Scouts passed along Lichfield Street flying the flag with patriotic pride in this march from the 1950s. The troop was connected with the grammar school founded in 1554 by Mary I, daughter of Henry VIII, for the 'education and improvement' of 66 local boys. The first location was in a small building on Church Hill. The school motto, 'What you give will be your only riches', could well have been transferred to the scouting movement. Modern cynics might scoff at scoutmasters with knobbly knees and little lads rubbing sticks together as they tried to light a camp fire around which they could sing jolly songs but they would be missing the point. The Boy Scout movement was founded in Great Britain in 1908 by a then cavalry officer, Lieutenant General Robert (later Lord) Baden-Powell, who had written a book called 'Scouting for Boys'. He was already well known as the defender of Mafeking in the Boer War. Baden-Powell's book described many games and contests that he had used to train cavalry troops in scouting. The scouting movement was aimed at boys from 11 to 14 or 15 years of age with the intention of developing in them good citizenship, chivalrous behaviour and skill in various outdoor activities. To become a scout a boy promised to be loyal to his country, help other people and in general obey the scouting code. What is there to scoff about in that?

The local elections to the Urban district Council were under way in Aldridge in 1960 and voters turned up in larger numbers than they do today, though this polling station was not as busy as it had been six months earlier for the general election of October 1959. Then, Harold Macmillan, or 'Supermac' as cartoonists christened him, had retained power as the Tory prime minister on a wave of optimism that the 1960s would continue the prosperity of the late 1950s. The mum casting her vote should have been proud of being able to pop her slip into the ballot box because her own mother could have been one of the strong minded band of women who campaigned so hard for equal rights. It had been only just over 30 years previously that the vote had been given to all women and it was important that that right was exercised. Later that year America would hold a general election for a new president. Macmillan's 'wind of change' that he described as sweeping through South Africa was to cross the Atlantic. John F Kennedy won a narrow victory over Richard Nixon and began a series of civil rights reforms that rocked racist society. Macmillan and Kennedy led their respective countries until late 1963. The British prime minister resigned after undergoing surgery and the American president died in a hail of bullets in Dallas.

Right: HRH Princess Alexandra has represented the Queen on numerous occasions, acting as a Counsellor of State in Her Majesty's absence abroad. In addition, she has made many official visits overseas, often accompanied by her husband. The Princess represented this country at the Nigerian independence celebrations in 1960, but in May 1961 she was strolling across the tarmac having arrived by helicopter to make a visit closer to home. She had come to Aldridge where she would find a district that had increased in population after World War II when businesses and people moved out of the crowded parts of Birmingham. New residential housing estates were built and industrial sites developed, adding to the image of a working environment that had existed there since the 19th century when lime works, coal mines and brickmaking abounded. Princess Alexandra was just 25 when she made this visit and, despite her privileged birth, had known sadness in her early life. Born on Christmas Day 1936, the second child of the Duke of Kent, she was just five years old when her father was killed in a wartime flying accident. Her upbringing, whilst not run of the mill, did not follow the more usual route for royalty of private governesses and education at home. She was the first British princess to go to an ordinary school when she enrolled at Heathfield School near Ascot.

Below: Ranks of children greeted Princess Alexandra warmly when she came to Middlemore Lane to open McKechnie Metal's works on 5 May 1961. Some of the youngsters were not completely sure who she was, but they had been informed that she was a royal princess and that was good enough for them. Anyone connected with the monarchy was an important person who deserved to be cheered so that she could report back to the Queen that the youth of Aldridge knew how to behave. The adults could have explained that Princess Alexandra was the Queen's first cousin and daughter of Princess Marina, another popular figure in royal circles. As a young woman Princess Alexandra made sure that she would have a wider knowledge of the world than some of her peers. On completing her education she took a nursing course at Great Ormond Street Hospital before starting to undertake official engagements. Her involvement in medicine has led to patronages that reflect this interest. She is the deputy president of the British Red Cross Society and the patron of the Alzheimer's Society, St Christopher's Hospice and Queen Alexandra's Royal Naval Nursing Service. The Princess is also known for her work for the blind and is the patron of the Guide Dogs for the Blind Association, Action for Blind People and the president of Sight Savers International. In 1962 she became engaged to Angus Ogilvy, marrying him on 24 April 1963 in Westminster Abbey.

Left: As the Rolls-Royce carrying Her Majesty hove into view necks were craned and people pressed forward to get a better look. Standing several deep the crowds lined the roads as Queen Elizabeth II paid her 1962 visit to the town. Many had waited patiently for hours so that they could get the best view. Children had rescued little union flags on sticks from the buckets they had used to make sand castles on the beach. Instead of sticking out of sand pies they were waved furiously as the entourage rolled past. Someone shouted for three cheers and hats were thrown into the air in celebration. It is now over 40 years since this visit, but many of us still have

that same fondness for royalty that we displayed back then. As the 20th century approached its final years it became fashionable to knock the royal family. To be fair, some of the antics of the Queen's children did not help, but the cynics were in a minority. The high regard in which the monarchy is held was well illustrated when the Queen Mother died in March 2002. Thousand upon thousand visited her lying in state and tuned into the televised funeral.

Below: When the Queen came to the Arboretum on 24 May 1962 in the 10th year of her reign hundreds of Girl Guides lined up for her inspection. They stood smartly to attention in the uniforms that their mothers had starched and ironed so carefully the night before. Standard bearers, with the name of each troop emblazoned on the fabric, proudly held their colours aloft. Queen Elizabeth II had been a keen guider in her younger days and enjoyed earning her badges in woodcraft, first aid and needlework just as keenly as any of those who had turned out to greet her. Becoming a Brownie is one of the fondest memories any girl has

of her childhood. It is having to make that special and solemn declaration of allegiance and obedience that ensures the formal joining of a pack is an achievement in its own right. Keeping the Brownie honour, working through the badges and getting ready to graduate to the Guides is part of growing up as a good little citizen, just as Robert Baden-Powell would have wanted. He and his sister Agnes started the movement in 1910 to complement the Boy Scouts, encouraging girls to be obedient, clean living and resourceful. Quite what the Baden-Powells would think of the baseball caps that Brownies now wear does not bear repetition, but at least the girls have remained true to the spirit of the movement.

Bottom: This was just one of many royal visits that have honoured Walsall. Here Queen Elizabeth II, elegant as ever in her pearls, suit and gloves, was about to sign the official visitors' book at the Council House on 24 May 1962. During her visit she took time to take in Crabtree's, the maker of electrical components upon whom she had also called in 1950, as had her late uncle George, Duke of Kent, in 1940. To mark her visit the founder's son, Mr J Crabtree, presented her with a piece of silverware. The Queen had been on the throne for 10 years and had built up a level of support and affection in her subjects that she must have found heartwarming. Despite her stilted style of speech, she appealed to the public as someone to whom it could relate for she was the mother of three young children. A fourth would be born two years after this visit. When her father died, thrusting her into the limelight at the tender age of 25, the nation fell in love with the young queen. It saw in her the new age of a monarchy that would mirror our recovery from the trials and tribulations of the postwar years as we built a new future for Britain.

his is why Americans love to visit Britain, for they have nothing like it in their own country. It is called heritage and ceremony. We have a thousand years of civilisation upon which to draw and when an important occasion needs to be marked we can give it all the pomp it deserves. That includes ceremonial dress, as displayed by the mayoral procession in 1969. A remembrance service had just been held and a wreath laid at the foot of the statue of Sister Dora. She holds a privileged position in the story of Walsall. Born Dorothy Wyndlow Pattison in 1832 in Yorkshire, this compassionate woman won the hearts of the Victorian town with her dedication in nursing and caring for the sick and

needy. She came to Walsall in 1865 and was involved in comforting and providing for grieving families at Pelsall colliery pithead. For five days they suffered, waiting for news of 22 men trapped underground. Sadly, all perished. She rolled up her sleeves and tended the dying at the Epidemic Hospital during the 1875 smallpox outbreak. Later that same year she looked after men horribly burned and disfigured after an explosion at an iron foundry. Her death in 1878 was a sad loss to the community. A statue to her was unveiled on The Bridge in 1886, affording her the honour that no other female, save a member of the royal family, had been given before. The original statue was replaced by a bronze cast in 1956.

At leisure

Blue Coat School was first mentioned when housed in an upper room over the old Market Cross at the top of High Street. There were 25 boys and 16 girls on the roll. The school later moved to The Bridge next to the George Hotel where the Walsall Observer later stood. In 1859 new buildings were found on St Paul's Street and Blue Coat School stayed there until 1934 before giving way to the new bus station. In 1939 children and staff were enjoying time at an adventure camp. It was a wonderful experience to be in the great outdoors, enjoying a camaraderie and taking part in a variety of activities designed to entertain and instruct them. Schools have always seen field trips, outward bound activities

and residential visits as valuable ways of widening their students' experiences. They are perhaps not as plentiful as they were before health and safety measures, trade union pressure, the national curriculum and less teacher free time began to limit the number of such ventures being undertaken. A poignant footnote to the Blue Coat adventure camp is that this was the last one to be held in peacetime for over six years. Did all these smiling faces survive the war or did some make the ultimate sacrifice in the service of their country? The modern Comprehensive Blue Coat School was built over King Street, in 1964-65. This street linked Ablewell Street with Birmingham Street and was the old road out of town.

Below centre: Trolley bus cables criss-crossed above the dome of Her Majesty's Theatre on Town End Bank. When it was built in 1900 Walsall already had the Imperial Theatre that opened in 1881 in the old Agricultural Hall, as well as the 1890 Grand on the corner of Park Street and Station Street. But, such was the Victorian demand for theatrical entertainment and love of music hall that Walsall could comfortably support another large enterprise. The new 2,000 seater theatre was opened by Sir William Pearman Smith and the curtain rose on its first production, 'Belle of New York'. Plays and pantomimes attracted some of the leading actors of the day, but Her Majesty's soon followed Edwardian trends and began turning its attention to variety shows. A young Charlie Chaplin once trod the boards here, but the introduction of talking pictures in the late 1920s demanded a rethink once again. This new fad swept the country and many theatres converted to cinemas to keep the cash registers ringing in their box offices. By 1933 Her Majesty's had followed suit. 'Rhythm on the Range', starring Bing Crosby, was on the bill in 1937. It was an easy going musical with a Western feel, but fell far short of the comic heights this popular crooner achieved when he teamed up with Bob Hope and Dorothy Lamour on the series of 'Road to' films during and after the war.

Bottom: ABC Cinemas purchased Her Majesty's Theatre on Town End Bank in April 1936. It had already been showing movies for three years when it changed hands, but the new owner decided to rebuild it as a purpose built cinema. It reopened as the Savoy on 3 October 1938, with the Mayor, Dr EC Drabble performing the official honours. The first film to be shown was entitled 'A Yank at Oxford', a rather prophetic title as several years later they would be everywhere, chewing their gum, dispensing nylon stockings and currying favour with the locals in their service uniforms. 'A Yank at Oxford' was a huge box office success with an all star cast that included Robert Taylor, Vivien Leigh, Lionel Barrymore and Maureen O'Sullivan. At that first showing audiences heard the voice of Neville Chamberlain on the newsreel, announcing that he had secured peace in our time after his meeting with Hitler in Munich. By the time this photograph of the Savoy was taken in 1956 cinema audiences had new worries being relayed to them via the crowing cockerel of Pathé News. It was the time of the Suez crisis that threatened our postwar economic recovery, just as we seemed to be turning the corner. Mario Lanza, an immensely popular tenor, was starring in 'Serenade'. The film's rags to riches story line about an opera singer played second fiddle to Lanza's magnificent singing voice. The Savoy was demolished in the late 1990s.

This was our first sight of the annual illuminations in the Arboretum that have twinkled away each year since 1952. The first exhibition was mounted by borrowing those lights that had wowed visitors to Blackpool. So popular did they prove with Walsall residents that the town was able to put on its own displays, attracting visitors and locals alike in the early autumn of each year. Only the Lancashire resort can now claim to have better known and more distinctive illuminations than these in the Arboretum. Those young at heart, whether toddlers or great grandparents, enjoy the imagination of the designers and the tableaux they create. Whether it be an illuminated Snow White or a brightly lit space rocket there are always oohs and aahs on the lips of each visitor. Now billed as 'the best free show in the Midlands', there was a delightful one off display mounted at the end of World War II. As part of the VE celebrations an illuminated caricature of Winston Churchill, complete with his trademark cigar, was mounted on a raft in the middle of the lake. Revellers danced under the lights until midnight. They were celebrating in the park created on the site of an old quarry, an idea originally mooted by the Walsall Arboretum and Lake Company, formed in 1870.

Far left: In 1954 nearly a decade had passed since peace was declared. Some of these children were the product of the baby boomer years that followed World War II and had been brought up in blissful ignorance of the fear that we often felt during the years of blackout and bombs. Their only awareness of wartime rigour came in the shape of rationing that was only just coming to an end. The adults behind them were not so carefree. A new threat was on the horizon in the shape of Russia and there was a very real worry that nuclear war was only just around the corner. Winston Churchill had coined the phrase 'iron curtain', referring to the screen of weaponry that the communists had stretched across eastern Europe. This period of history became known as the cold war and civil defence groups continued to organise drills and practise evacuation procedures just in case the mushroom clouds came to Britain instead of Hiroshima and Nagasaki. It was said that we would have a four minute warning in the event of nuclear attack so, realistically, we would never have had time to react well enough. This defence day exercise took place in Memorial Park, Willenhall. The park had opened in 1922 in honour of those lost in the 1914-18 war on reclaimed derelict land and boasted a particularly fine bandstand that was a big attraction.

Left: Children just love a trip to the park. Even now with all their electronic games, DVDs and cartoon videos they still love to jump on a roundabout, whiz down a slide and swing as high as they possibly can. In April 1969 they could also visit the children's lido, though it was a brave soul who dipped a toe into the water at that time of year. The first stage of the new attraction in the Arboretum was opened in the summer of 1953. Much of the funding had been raised by drawing on the profits from the annual two day horticultural show and fête. The event that year had been blessed with good weather, swelling the crowds who commented that it was the first one that they had been to in 13 years when the heavens had not opened. Over 30,000 packed the grounds and many only had the smallest glimpse of Berlita, an ice skating star of the day, perform the opening ceremony. Within minutes of the ribbon being cut the pools were packed. This was despite the polio scare that had seen a falling off of attendances in swimming baths and paddling pools as some parents forbade their children frequenting such places. They were frightened that they would contract the crippling disease that was not countered by the Salk vaccine until the late 1950s.

New homes for old

It's getting harder every day to recall now just how tired and run down some of our townscape looked 30 or 40 years ago. Since that time many older buildings have been demolished to make way for the new. And more recently greater emphasis has been placed on refurbishing older buildings to grant them a new lease of life, bringing them up to modern standards whilst preserving their architectural merits. That process has occurred all over Britain, throughout Walsall, and especially in Caldmore.

Caldmore is just one of the many urban villages which developed around the town centre of Walsall over the past two hundred years. However, in the early 1970s, unlike the others Caldmore had its own village green (now a traffic island) as a focal point; a green which had been overlooked by a fine Jacobean Mansion House since the mid sixteenth century. This was once the home of the Hawes family, but since the mid

nineteenth century the building had been the White Hart public house.

Through two centuries of industrial, commercial and residential development the once rural and quiet pastures of Caldmore have been transformed into a noisy urban centre with heavy industry providing local

Right: *A meeting of the Caldmore Residents Association in the early 1970s.* **Below:** *Caldmore Green pictured in 1963.*

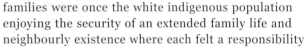

employment and terraced streets housing a vigorous working class community.

Although situated only half a mile from the centre of Walsall the people of Caldmore have rarely had to take the journey into town for in the commercial life which surrounds the Green were shops selling every variety of wares, a number of pubs owned by different breweries, local political clubs and churches of almost every denomination.

The long terraced streets leading into the centre like spokes on the hub of a wheel, provided both the living and playing spaces for the many large families which made up the street communities. The

Top: A festival scene dated 1974, the Bakers Arms and the Housing Advice Centre can be seen in the background.
Above: *Fundraising activities in the 1970s. Mrs Blower is to the right of the picture.*

families were once the white indigenous population enjoying the security of an extended family life and neighbourly existence where each felt a responsibility for the other and where money was so scarce it had long been dispensed with as a means of bringing happiness. By the late twentieth century however a variety of people from many different cultures, still relatively impoverished, were living harmoniously together in one community in the village of Caldmore.

During much of the long history of Caldmore as an urban village the housing stock had remained comparatively good; a fact borne out by the number of large, sturdy pre-1919 properties still in existence. Even so by the late 1960s many of those houses, either through neglect by absent landlords, or through sheer wear and tear, became unfit for human habitation, with a large proportion having no bathroom or inside toilet.

The community itself was also becoming aged, with children moving away to take opportunities elsewhere, leaving newly arrived Commonwealth immigrants to work in the lower paid heavy industries alongside a static, older workforce. The immigrants had to live in homes which were rapidly deteriorating and for which they often paid exorbitant prices to unscrupulous vendors. The Local Authority's neglect of individual needs as well as the general environment of Caldmore only served to accelerate the rundown of the area, and in particular its housing stock.

The cumulative effect of these factors raised people's indignation and when the Council failed to respond to a request for the clearance of a rat-infested site in the heart of the area a group of residents came together to bring joint action against the Council. They first met on 17th September 1970 and the Caldmore Residents Action Group (CRAG) was formed to deal with both individual cases and the larger environmental issues.

Pressure from the CRAG managed to convince Walsall Council to declare a General Improvement Area, a Housing Action Area and a Rolling Programme for Redevelopment in Caldmore in addition to numerous other environmental improvement projects. To lend support to these new projects CRAG formed itself into five different Area Committees on which each street or tower block had a representative who collected a pre-decimal sixpence each Friday from the residents within their area. CRAG was entirely funded in this way and the residents' news sheet (The Local Gossip) was paid for from those subscriptions.

Trust and the Caldmore Area Housing Association Limited at 13 Caldmore Green.

The first Board of the Caldmore Housing Association was formed under the chairmanship of Dr Cornwall, the Principal of the West Midlands College of Education, in 1972. Its first two properties were bought with a loan of just £400 from the Walsall Borough Council. Two years later Caldmore Housing built 30 new flats at Newmore Gardens.

The Act Aid Trust was formed in 1973 to attract charitable funds to the work that was now taking place, and Shelter (the Campaign for the Homeless) and the Cadbury Trust became early benefactors. The Trust members comprised the Chairman and Secretary of CRAG in addition to the Secretaries of the five Area Committees so providing continuity.

The front room of CRAG Chairman, Bert Blower, at 29 Victor Street was originally used as an office/drop in centre; these premises were superseded by the first Registered Offices of the Act Aid

Above right: *Lower Rushall Street seen before development in 1976.* **Right:** *The same area in September 1980, with Jervis Court and Wollaston Court providing homes for 107 single people.*

The Trust's first act was to use its funds to buy an empty shop in the heart of Caldmore and convert it into Walsall's first Housing Aid Centre. From there CRAG was also managed and in 1973 Barrie Blower, one of the originators of the Action Group, was employed as a Housing Aid worker. Areas of severe housing need were now being identified, which included many Special Needs categories which Caldmore Area Housing Association Limited was to deal with later.

The informal way of handling problems in a drop-in centre setting, coupled with the idea that these Centres should belong to local people certainly influenced Walsall Council in its Decentralisation Programme which resulted in the town's numerous Neighbourhood Offices.

On a lighter side the CRAG and Act Aid Committee Members and Voluntary Workers became increasingly involved in organising a wide variety of community activities: seaside trips, special outings for children and the elderly and a four day village festival involving all the community would become annual events.

Top: *Young people learning building skills on a Manpower Services Commission scheme, 1982.*
Above: *The Peace Party in 1985.*

Much of Act Aid's work would be absorbed into the Caldmore Housing Association in 1980 when charitable donations were no longer available.

A Local Authority Health Survey in 1961 had revealed that 70 per cent of the houses on Caldmore were unfit for human habitation. It was that report and the Local Authority's failure to act upon it that led to the formation of the Caldmore Residents Action Group in 1970 and sowed the seeds for the formation of the Caldmore Area Housing Association Limited (CAHAL) two years later. The fact that the area had so many hundreds of substantially unfit homes serves to demonstrate the task that CAHAL faced following its incorporation on 12th June 1972. Its role was to complement and assist the Local Authority in tackling that high level of deprivation, which became the major platform of its work. It was also important that the Action Group and Act Aid Trust remained involved in those early years, as the area had been undergoing change from the mid 1960s, with large numbers of families from the Indian subcontinent moving in and adding their contributions to the evolving community.

The Caldmore Housing Association was formed to provide help in achieving bricks and mortar solutions to homelessness and bad housing. Obviously managing a large borrowing agency such as a housing association required a number of different skills and the first shareholders were knowledgeable local people such as traders, industrialists and church leaders. The Act Aid Trust and the Caldmore Residents Action Group were also represented, as were people from the different ethnic groups to provide a carefully balanced community input. The Steering Group first met in 1971 and the Association acquired its first properties, two houses in the General Improvement Area, at the end of 1972.

There were several hundred homes in Caldmore and the surrounding areas which needed rehabilitation, as well as many derelict infill sites to be brought into residential use. The 1974 Housing Act gave a spur to the activities of housing associations and Caldmore Housing was quick to grasp that opportunity. Special Needs also became of importance in providing homes to meet the needs of those requiring short-term accommodation while going through a transitional period in their lives - such as women suffering from domestic violence, vagrants, former psychiatric patients and various other 'at risk' groups. Tackling these problems to great effect would make Caldmore Housing a national leader as a community based housing association and make it highly respected for its work locally.

Meanwhile CRAG's work was finally taken over by the Act Aid Trust in 1975, but not before it had become recognised as the largest group of its kind in the country, and certainly the most active outside London.

Top right: *The old White Hart public house, the second oldest building in Caldmore, being given a new lease of life as association flats. The Heritage Centre is housed on the top floor.*
Above right: *The opening of the first purpose built dwellings for Asian elderly at Apna Ghar, Pleck, Walsall in 1988.*

In 1976 so much activity was going on locally that the BBC produced a half hour documentary on the work of the Association in a film entitled 'Caldmore Rises'.

The Association however has never stood still and was always looking for new ways of serving both its tenants and their neighbours within the community. For ten years, from 1977 it sponsored Manpower Service Commission schemes which helped to train young people in a variety of different building trades. It also acted as a sponsor to Manpower Service Commission schemes where adults were employed on a number of initiatives within the Community Enterprise Programme and Community Programmes. Such activities would result in the Association opening a Training Centre at Hollemeadow Avenue to provide training for 120 youths in Building, Decorating, Motor Mechanics, Carpentry and other skills.

During their sponsorship many of the Housing Association's tenants and young people benefited from employment on these Manpower Services Commission schemes.

Work continued in a variety of areas. In 1979 for example an Afro-Caribbean Hostel was opened with revenue support from Walsall MBC and the Home Office. In 1980 Second Caldmore Area Housing Association was formed to act as a sister organisation to carry out Low Cost/Shared Ownership schemes. That same year Royal recognition was forthcoming with HRH the Duke of Edinburgh coming to

Caldmore to officiate at the opening of Wollaston/ Jervis Court, two blocks of flats which provided homes for over a hundred single people. The following year the Association was also housing Vietnamese people in a short life property scheme.

By 1983, just ten years after its first two properties had been bought, the Association was employing 500 adults on 22 different community projects, including an Urban Farm, Canal Museum, Visiting the Elderly, recycling furniture, waste and clothing projects on its Manpower Services Commission Community Programme schemes.

When the numbers became too large in 1984 the Association formed a sister company called CAUSE Limited (the Caldmore Urban Support Enterprise Ltd), a non profit making body which took on responsibility for training. CAUSE would become a totally independent company later renamed Cause Training Workshops Limited but still continued to carry on the work which the Caldmore Area Housing Association initiated all those years ago.

More royal Recognition was to follow in 1986 with HRH Diana, Princess of Wales officiating at the opening of the Association's project for the deaf in Lichfield Street, whilst the following year the Association opened a drop-in centre in Countess Street offering leisure facilities for over 100 Asian elders.

Top right: *HRH Diana, Princess of Wales is greeted by Caldmore Area HA Chairman, Richard Newby, and Chief Executive, Barrie Blower, as she opens the Association's Project for the Deaf in Lichfield Street.*
Left: *Don Maclean officiates at the opening of the St Catherine's Elderly Persons Scheme in Walsall with from left; Father Harrington, David Matthews (Caldmore Area HA Chairman), Lady Mayoress, Barrie Blower and Mayor Norman Matthews.*

The Association's first purpose built dwellings for Asian elderly were opened at Apna Ghar in Pleck in 1988. The following year the Association moved to its present offices, the former cinema at 18 Caldmore Green.

After twenty years the Caldmore Housing Association had become a large landlord in a small area, and although still in need of resources, it endeavoured through all its activities to be responsive and accountable to local people, continuing to retain the ethos of the Voluntary Housing Movement. In 1992 some £2.75 million of private finance money was raised from the Bradford & Bingley Building Society; with those funds the Association began work with the Bethany Project in Stafford to produce units for single homeless people - this would be the only development the Housing Association would own outside Walsall. But Walsall was not forgotten: the next year the Association, in partnership with Accord Housing, developed a mixed tenure scheme of 98 units on the former Sister Dora Hospital site. The Sister Dora Hospital had opened in 1878 as the Walsall Cottage Hospital. The building was renamed the Sister Dora Hospital in 1879 following the death of Dorothy Wyndlow Pattison, 'Sister Dora', a well loved nursing sister who had worked in Walsall since 1865 and who had been constantly involved in the planning and detailing of the then new building to provide the best possible health care for the people of Walsall. The Health Authority decided that the old building was surplus to its requirements in 1991.

During excavation for the houses two time capsules were uncovered which provided a social record dating back to the time of the original construction. The documents from the capsule were donated to Walsall Local History Museum. The Association incorporated a new time capsule under the new development to give future generations similar insight.

Design and conservation would be daunting tasks at the hospital site. Use of the site was constrained by significant changes in level, massive retaining walls, trees which had to be preserved and a building facade that had to be retained and built into the new design. The character of the original building would be recreated by the inclusion of finials, gables, pyramid roofs, gate posts and an entire facade was copied as new three storey housing. The total cost of the project would be £4.5 million.

Although the hospital has disappeared forever Sister Dora and her connection with the site would be preserved by naming part of the scheme the Sister Dora Gardens.

Top left: Page one from the brochure commemorating the opening of the Sister Dora Housing Project in October 1985. ***Above right:*** *The Chat Shop at 39 Caldmore Green, which opened in 1994 selling second hand goods.* ***Right:*** *The Xchange at Caldmore Green, formerly the Bakers Arms, but now a Community Resource Centre, providing a Nursery, Parents & Tots group and meeting rooms.*

which owned nearly 2,000 homes costing over £71 million. Annual income from rents alone would be more than £5.5 million a year with £1.2 million being spent annually on the maintenance of the large property portfolio.

Those 'big business' numbers however would not lead to the Association losing sight of its primary objectives: to provide a choice of appropriate homes to those in the greatest need; to assist in the alleviation of poverty; to join with other agencies with similar aims; to identify and meet its 'stakeholders' hopes and needs and to train and develop its staff within a caring environment - and to provide resources, facilities, amenities and practical support to both the Association's tenants and the community in which they live.

Meanwhile the Association also opened its tenant-managed 'CHAT' shop at 39 Caldmore Green selling second-hand goods.

In a more dramatic move 1995 saw the Housing Association convert the old White Hart pub, Walsall's second oldest building, for use as flats, with the upper floor being used as a museum.

The late 1990s would be a period of continuing innovation with the Association developing its largest ever estate, composed entirely of houses, at Hatherton Road where 46 new houses were built in 1997, the Association's Silver Jubilee year. In the last year of the old century 25 flats were created for sale over shops in Station Street.

By the early years of the new millennium, from its small start some 30 years earlier, the Caldmore Area Housing Association had grown enormously. From its modest beginnings the Association had grown into an organisation

Since the 1960s the streets of Walsall and Caldmore in particular have seen extraordinary changes. Many of us remember those days with affection, but few of us would want to return to the days of coal fires instead of central heating or exchange our indoor bathrooms for outside toilets.

Some communities were of course in worse condition than others. Caldmore was then a tired, worn out community with hundreds of sub standard homes. Few would want to live there today had things not changed. Fortunately the will, and determination of a few far sighted individuals energised the community; a process which would see sustained improvements being made not just for one year or even ten but down all the decades since.

The community itself succeeded where local government failed, deciding that in the words once used by Royalty 'something must be done'. Many individuals contributed to the regeneration of Caldmore both in small ways and large ways. But few contributed more than those who acted as midwives to the Caldmore Area Housing Association, an organisation which, more than any other, would be responsible for turning Caldmore round from being an area in terminal decline to one in which its residents could feel proud to live.

Top left: The signing ceremony at the Sister Dora project, 1995. Above left: Members of the Board and staff celebrate the Investors in People Award in 1996. Right: Chief Executive Barrie Blower.

Bird's eye view

Worshippers have been able to say their prayers in the church here since the beginning of the 13th century. The old Blue Coat Infants School, demolished in February 1963, is to the right and the former Brotherhood building can be seen just below St Matthew's Church on the corner of the memorial gardens. The Brotherhood was built as a social club and boasted a fine billiards room. The gardens were designed by Geoffrey Jellicoe in 1950-51, just one of a series of magnificent projects undertaken by the landscape artist who was also responsible for the grounds of the Royal Lodge at Windsor, the Kennedy Memorial at Runnymede and Sutton Place near Guildford, Surrey. Jellicoe was as important to the 20th century as Capability Brown was to the 18th. He was knighted for his services in 1979. The church has been remodelled over the years and some evidence of this can be seen in the preservation of the original 13th century inner crypt, the 15th century red sandstone of the chancel and 19th century white stone. Major restoration work took place in 1819-21, but some unexpected internal refurbishment was required in 1847. A church beadle decided to investigate the source of a smell of gas. His decision to use a candle to light his way resulted in the inevitable. The explosion not only blew away the windows but his own existence as well.

In the foreground of this bird's eye view of the town we can clearly see the railway lines that helped boost Walsall's economy in the 19th century. The canal system had already assisted industry to access wider markets across the midlands, but the coming of the locomotive opened up the whole country. This gave the great upsurge in the fortunes of heavier industry that was to be the backbone of the town's development. Workers flocked into Walsall, pushing up the population, and factory and business owners smiled as their profit and loss accounts grew ever more healthy. In 1825 Stockton and Darlington had the first passenger line, followed by the Liverpool to Manchester service that was inaugurated in 1830. The opening of the Grand Junction Railway from Birmingham to Warrington in 1837 meant that the area was in the early vanguard of this pioneering form of travel and transportation. A station was built at Bescot Bridge and by 1846 the South Staffordshire Railway had brought the town into the main system, opening its station at Bridgeman Place. This latter one was only a temporary measure as it was replaced by a new one built on the newly formed Station Street two years later. Initially rail travel was an expensive business. A first class return to Birmingham cost half a crown, but fares fell in the second half of the 19th century bringing the railways within reach of the masses.

There used to be pasture in the foreground for horses to graze upon and stables where they could rest before setting off on their daily work, but that was long before this view across Walsall was taken. Something of that long lost time has been retained in the name of the spot from where we are looking because this is the site on Paddock Lane on where more buildings would rise. Motorists would soon have to find somewhere else to park their cars as the development began to take shape. In the 1960s planners decided that new housing for an increasing population would use space better if homes went up from rather than across available building land. The era of the high rise tower blocks was born. Unfortunately, architects failed to appreciate that these would lead to a drop in community spirit and that the morale of some residents would suffer as they felt marooned several floors above terra firma. The chimneys and factories in the distance act as a good reminder that Walsall's prosperity from an early date was based on local supplies of coal, iron ore, and limestone. By the 17th century Walsall was an important industrial town with its saddlery, nail and iron manufactures and still boasts of playing a major role as a thriving industrial centre, important for lock and key making, nuts and bolts as well as its famed leather related products.

Wartime

A motorised military is, of course, a 20th century phenomenon. That is what it might well remain because air supremacy has taken over as the vital aspect of any modern conflict, even if tanks still roll in urban areas. At the start of World War I there were still some cavalry units and horses were sometimes being used to drag cannon and heavy equipment. However, a mounted charge against a line of entrenched troops armed with rapid firing small arms was suicidal. Cavalry organisations soon abandoned horses for armoured vehicles and became known as mechanised cavalry or armoured cavalry. Tanks first played a decisive role in the Battle of Cambrai in 1917 when 474 British tanks broke through the German lines and they were used in increasing numbers by the Allies in that war. The officers inspecting the line of military vehicles knew that progress across Europe in World War II relied heavily upon the support that could be given to the advancing troops. It was no good pushing on unless supplies of food, equipment and ammunition could rapidly be replenished. Fleets of lorries, backed up by armoured personnel carriers, were needed to move large stocks quickly and efficiently. When these officers were boys the Army's horses needed fodder. The modern steeds required oil in their feeding troughs.

Below: Who do you think you are kidding, Mr Hitler? The Bloxwich Home Guard had no intention of letting some foreign predator eat away at the heart of Britain. They were ready to stand firm if the invasion ever came and, in the meantime, lend a hand on other civil defence duties. The highly popular TV sitcom of the 1970s, 'Dad's Army', did these men little justice. Whilst it was very funny, it tended to belittle the work and dedication of these volunteers. It is true that in the early days of the Local Defence Volunteers there were instances of drills being carried out by men marching with broomsticks across their shoulders, but by the time they were renamed the Home Guard in July 1940 things had changed. Lt Parkes, Major Wilkes, Lt Talbot and 2nd Lt Ball, pictured towards the end of the front row, and the rest of the Bloxwich parade turned

themselves into a professional unit. This unit held its first ceremonial parade on 27 July 1940 and, when the bombs began to fall, respect began to grow accordingly. They were not alone in the good work being carried out. St John Ambulance, the Red Cross and members of the Women's Voluntary Service all put the needs of their fellows first. We had ATS and Land Army girls more than just doing their bit. All in all they became part of what Churchill referred to as 'the army that Hitler forgot'.

Bottom: During the war parish and town boundaries became blurred when the need arose. It was all part of the community spirit that bonded us as a nation during the dark hours. When a cry for help was heard we answered as quickly as we could. On 14 November 1940 the call came from Coventry when enemy bombers, as part of the German blitz on provincial Britain, hammered the city. We had beaten back the fighter planes in the skies over southern England during the Battle of Britain in the late summer, but now the attempt to crush our industries and our will had begun in earnest. These men and their vehicle were part of the rescue team sent to help the people of Coventry pick up the pieces after a night of terror that had left over 1,000 people dead and many thousands of buildings, including St Michael's cathedral, wrecked beyond repair. The scene of carnage that awaited the rescue teams gave them nightmares that would return for years to come. Sifting through rubble and debris in the search for survivors presented the potential shock of coming across an arm or leg no longer part of anything recognisable. Is it any wonder that, having coped with such horrors, many refused to talk about their experiences afterwards? Six days after the raid on Coventry the Luftwaffe returned and pounded Birmingham and neighbouring districts the whole night long.

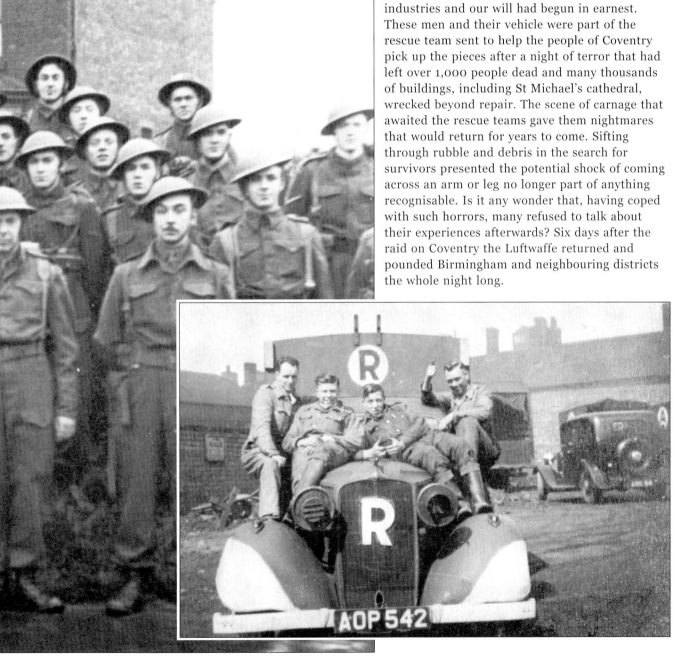

Below: Bunkers, cellars, underground railways and vaults were all pressed into service as hidey holes from enemy air raids in World War II. Many of us also had special shelters at the end of the garden or on a spot of waste land nearby. John Anderson was the Home Secretary who introduced these corrugated steel structures buried in the ground. Families put candles, blankets and emergency rations inside them to keep them going as the Junkers and Heinkels flew overhead. Anderson shelters were free to those with low incomes and the breathing space provided by the phoney war enabled households to prepare their own defences. Babies had their own special gas masks that looked like deep sea divers' helmets. Blackout curtains were hung and children evacuated to the countryside, though many were homesick and soon returned. Later in the war another form of shelter, named after another Home Secretary, was added to the list of precautions. The Morrison shelter was meant for indoor use and resembled a reinforced table. In addition to these personal precautions was the assistance provided by members of the ARP. The Air Raid Wardens' service was created in 1937 and Walsall formed its own branch the following year. Initial apathy caused only 850 to volunteer by June 1938, but the Munich crisis encouraged an upsurge in applications to join the service.

The World War II soldiers took a few minutes out to relax and pose for the camera. Smoking was one way of relieving the tension and a 'coffin nail' helped them wind down before returning to their duties. Some took it easy with a game of cards or enjoyed looking at a photograph of a loved one or perhaps a pin up of Betty Grable or a scantily clad Jane. The latter was a forces' favourite cartoon strip character who always seemed to have problems keeping her clothing in order. Those far from home were always anxious to receive a letter and the ones they sent back were usually full of hope and good cheer. It was not the done thing to be pessimistic and, anyway, the censor's blue pencil would have struck through suggestions that the war was not going well. They agonised about how wives and sweethearts were managing and secretly fretted that a 'Dear John' letter might be coming their way. Friendships forged during those days often lasted long after peace was declared. Men who had shared billets and bullets in close proximity to one another formed bonds that could never be broken. Some were more reserved, but not because they were unfriendly. They were wary of becoming too close to someone who might go out one day and never return.

Queen Street throbbed with joyous activity and cheerful celebrations as the residents celebrated VE Day. Victory in Europe had taken nearly six years to achieve and all that the children preparing to tuck in could remember of their young lives was that they were ones touched by shortages, fear and sadness. They were growing up surrounded by ration coupons, bomb craters and missing relatives. But those troubles were put to one side as they prepared to party. Every street in the country was like this one, bedecked with flags and bunting flying above trestle tables that had been borrowed from schools and church halls. Mums had pooled their meagre rations or blown a week's worth of food coupons to put on the best spread the children had ever feasted upon. The buns might have been on the dry side as egg powder was not quite the same as the real thing, but they were buns after all. It was all far better than that revolting pie of swedes, turnips and parsnips that Lord Woolton recommended. We can be sure he never tasted it. After the celebratory tea someone found an old wind up gramophone and put on a record of the hokey-cokey and everyone danced himself silly. Whilst they cleared away the mothers sang quietly about bluebirds and Dover, shedding a small tear for those who never made it back for this or any other party.

Above: 'Drinking our beer and chatting up our women,' thought the old chap as he concentrated on his own tankard, ignoring the GIs enjoying their drinks. He had seen it all before in the first world war and the Americans were back again. The slang term 'GI' for an American soldier comes from the abbreviation for government issue, referring to their uniforms and equipment. Although we begrudged them their wads of cash and the brashness they displayed we had to admit that we could not have won the war without their help. America only entered in late 1941 after the Japanese attack on Pearl Harbour, but by November 1942 its troops were fighting alongside ours in North Africa. By the time of this 1944 photograph there were American

300,000 personnel to enemy action in all campaigns and, despite the initial misgivings about their arrogance, we have to admit that their contribution was immense. The co-operation that Churchill and Roosevelt showed during the war was continued by their successors in government during peacetime.

Top: Now we could really put the war to rest and little Johnny could truly sleep in his own little room again. For too many years he had come into mum's room, too frightened of the dark and the threat of the bombs to stay on his own. The war in Europe had ended in May 1945, but still rumbled on in the Far East until Japan at last threw in the towel. The cause of her capitulation was horrendous, 120,000 inhabitants of Hiroshima and Nagasaki being killed when atomic bombs vaporised the cities in August. Radiation was to affect the lives of many more over the coming years, but the Allies had been spared further casualties in the field when Emperor Hirohito accepted defeat. In the Old Barn Community Centre at Pheasey they celebrated the news with a VJ party, just as we all did in on streets and in halls across the rest of the country. Bonfires burned from every vantage point in the land and crowds danced giant conga chains in the roads. There were still worries for some because their loved ones were in Japanese POW camps and the sights of the inmates liberated from the German death camps in Buchenwald, Auschwitz, Dachau and Belsen were still fresh in their minds. Their worst fears were realised when seriously emaciated prisoners who had been working as slave labour on the Siam to Burma railroad were discovered. They were the lucky ones because thousands had already died from starvation or disease.

bases in this country flying bombing missions into Germany and preparing men for the Allied invasion on D-Day, 6 June when the Normandy landings started to turn the tide. The US Army lost many men on the beaches codenamed Utah and Omaha, but their sacrifices brought a growing respect from those of us back home. The American combined services lost nearly

On the move

Cobbled streets and tram tracks from the days of some threequarters of a century ago when variety was the name of transport in 1927. There were still some horse drawn vehicles on the road, the old vying with the new as motor cars also trundled their way along Bridge Street. The tram belonged to that transitional era from four legged to four wheeled transport. Bicycles were a common sight as both a mode of personal transport and for the use of delivery boys taking purchases from the shops to a customer's home. Bridge Street was constructed in 1766, making a new link towards Birmingham known initially as the New Road. The photograph was taken at a time when Britain was supposed to be reaping the rewards of a land fit for heroes that the government had promised after the Great War drew to an end in late 1918. They were fine words but provided little in substance. By 1926 the country's workers, maddened by wage cuts, longer hours and failed promises, took to the streets in the General Strike. The following year unemployed miners from the Rhondda marched 180 miles to London, rallying in Trafalgar Square. Prime minister Baldwin refused to meet them, continuing the existence of a 'them and us' culture that bedevilled our nation in those years that led us into the depression that meant starvation and despair for the families of heroes who had given their all on the Somme and at Ypres.

Above: Quite a dicey manoeuvre was being carried out on Bloxwich High Street in the late 1960s that would have led to a quick warning toot on the horn. Perhaps you could say that the car in the middle of the road was 'heralding' a potential accident. Today it would probably bring a pitched bout of fisticuffs as violent road rage seems to have replaced the raised eyebrow. Once upon a time Bloxwich would not have encountered such potential problems. Named after the Bloc family and recorded in the Domesday Book as Blocheswic (Bloc's village) it was a quiet agricultural hamlet in medieval times. The opening of the coal mines in the 18th century and the development of a number of cottage industries that included nail and needle making assisted in its expansion. But it grew beyond recognition after the second world war. Three new housing estates, built in the 1950s and 1960s, completely changed its character. High Street is often congested with traffic today as vehicles head up the A34 towards Cannock and the A5. Certainly the man crossing the road in the centre of the picture would not now be able to stroll sedately across. Instead it would be a case of head down, close your eyes and make a dash for it.

Right: Hospital Street links the A34 Green Lane with Stafford Street at the point that the latter becomes Bloxwich Road. This street had been known as Deadman's Lane for centuries. The borough's Epidemic Hospital was established here in 1872 at a cost of £2,000 and, unfortunately, because of the nature of the diseases and the primitive medicines available the road lived up to its name. Sister Dora spent some time nursing in the hospital, being particularly praiseworthy for her work during the smallpox epidemic. There were six wards for infectious cases and two convalescent areas, figures that suggest that many moved from the main wards and into the cemetery rather than into recovery. There was accommodation for the nurses on site that acted as both serving their needs and protecting the public on the outside. The hospital was last used during an outbreak of diphtheria in 1924-25 and was later to become the site for William Bate's factory. As the trolley bus made its way along Hospital Street passengers unaware of the hospital's history would not have given a second thought to the wonders of penicillin, inoculations, antibiotics and vaccines available to them on the NHS. The main letters available to Sister Dora were TLC (tender loving care).

'Gone fishin', put a sign above the door', as Bing Crosby and Louis Armstrong once duetted. Although this was probably staged for the benefit of the camera, the British Rail porter had little else to do with his time when floodwater hit Walsall yet again. Despite all the technology that had put Armstrong and Aldrin on the surface of the moon in 1969 mankind had still not found a way to hold back the rains that made life a misery whenever it poured down at a rate with which the storm drains could not cope. It seems laughable that a few years later the government would appoint Denis Howells as the Minister for Drought. The businessman in his suit, crossword at the ready, does not seem to have noticed that it is unlikely that his 8.21 to Birmingham will be leaving on time. He is taking it all rather stoically, but he is British after all. In the meantime the porter fished on, dreaming of the days when little branch lines and rural stations still operated. Then along came Dr Beeching and his blueprint for streamlining the rail network. He did not just remodel it as butcher it. Big was beautiful and the small country stations and the lines that serviced them were taken out of service.

Below: Darby and Joan, Becks and Posh or Antony and Cleopatra. Pay your money and take your choice, but this pair had a togetherness as their development dominated our roads for decades. Austin and Morris are two of the most famous names in the annals of motoring history from the last century. The van belonged to the company begun by Henry Austin at Longbridge in 1906. He drew on his early experience working for the Wolseley Sheep Shearing Company to create the Austin Seven that greatly influenced British and European light car design. William Morris began his career in the motor transport industry with motorbikes, before establishing car production with the Morris Oxford at Cowley. Austin and Morris joined forces in 1952 as the British Motor Corporation, though they kept their own names within the company. The Morris Minor in the picture was one of the best selling family saloons of that time, remaining in production from 1948 to 1971. A reliable car with excellent steering and cornering qualities, it was the first all British car to pass the 1,000,000 mark in sales. The vehicles were photographed on Portland Street in 1964, a road once known as Hammerforge Lane where bits and stirrups had formerly been manufactured in workrooms at the rear of houses. It was renamed after the Duke of Portland of Warbeck Abbey. The Oak Tanning Company building is in the background.

Top: This 1969 picture shows the trolley bus departure platform at the bus station on St Paul's Street that opened in 1935 on a site where Blue Coat School used to stand. This bus station was demolished in 1970 to make way for a new, improved version that in its turn gave way to the ambitiously designed model we have today. It is situated close to the church that has now been converted into shops, restaurants and a conference centre. Trams, of course, were the first vehicles to be used in large scale public transport. Electrified lines were run as early as 1892. By the inter war years many of the old tracks were becoming badly worn and trolley buses were seen as a viable alternative as they could use much of the existing cabling whilst doing away with the need for tramlines. The swinging arms of these buses, reaching high overhead, soon became a common sight. They were not introduced without some controversy, however. Pedestrians took a while to get used to their being on the roads as the old trams gave good warning of their arrival on the scene by the clanking and clattering they made. Trolley buses moved much more quietly and there were a number of accidents to people caught unawares. To some they became known as 'the creeping death'. As they lacked the flexibility of movement that motor buses had, hooked as they were to overhead power, hold ups often occurred at notorious bottlenecks. One of the worst of these was at Town End Bank where traffic was often at a standstill.

Above right: Park Street is now pedestrianised and with Digbeth and part of High Street provides a continuous shopping street for Walsall residents. In May 1969 it was still open to traffic, as can be seen from this view taken from the new shopping precinct. This was the part of the early days of the changes that altered shopping styles in most town centres. Large chain stores flexed their muscles and smaller, individual businesses found competition fierce. As the pace of life quickened we wanted to make our purchases swiftly and centrally, so indoor arcades and centres replaced the traditional promenade along the street from shop to shop.

Park Street gained its name as it led to an old park and was mentioned in documents dating right back to 1247. The park was not one of swings and roundabouts but a large expanse of woodland where deer roamed free. An impressive Georgian building Park Hall erected in 1775, once stood near Town End Bank. As the 1960s drew to a close shoppers had little interest in the fine old buildings of yesteryear or the noble animals that once ran wild amongst the trees. They needed to buy their Surprise peas, packets of Omo and bottles of Babycham, load them into their Ford Anglias and get off home to their little boxes on a housing estate.

Far right: Corporation trolley bus No 861 on Proffitt Street in 1969 would only have another year of service to give. It seems ironic that Proffitt Street leads towards Ryecroft Cemetery as the days of this form of public transport were numbered. By the start of World War II Walsall had built up a fleet of 200 buses that include 21 trolleys. After the war significant additions were made, notably when 10 new four wheeler Sunbeams were bought in 1951, each carrying 56 passengers. By the mid 1950s longer wheelbased vehicles were introduced and new routes to housing estates at Blakenall, Bloxwich and Bentley were established. By 1959 the number of trolley buses had risen to 47, peaking at 63 in 1963. However, this form of transport had insurmountable problems when the M6 motorway was constructed across the Walsall to Willenhall route. Rising electricity costs and road congestion added further nails

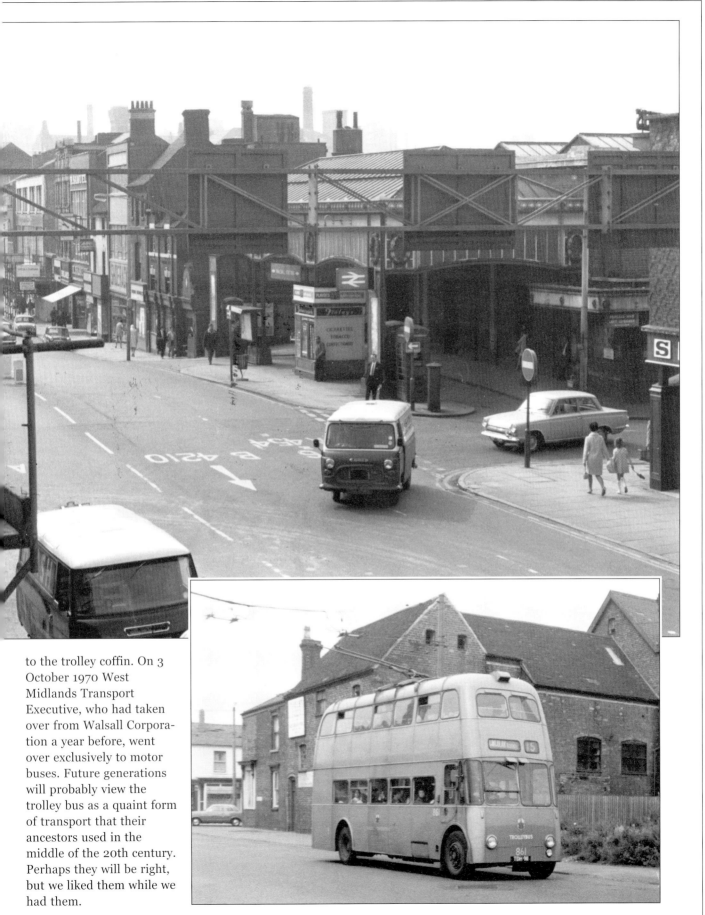

to the trolley coffin. On 3 October 1970 West Midlands Transport Executive, who had taken over from Walsall Corporation a year before, went over exclusively to motor buses. Future generations will probably view the trolley bus as a quaint form of transport that their ancestors used in the middle of the 20th century. Perhaps they will be right, but we liked them while we had them.

Shopping spree

Standing on the corner of Bridge Street in 1935 if people were keeping their eyes peeled for the next tram to come along the tracks that swept away in front of them then they were going to be disappointed. The last one had left two years earlier. Just for a short while the streets had hummed to the sound of three different types of public transport as motor buses, trams and trolley buses worked side by side. The first electrified tram service ran in 1892, though there had been horse drawn cars for some years before then. Some of those standing around on Bridge Street had nothing better to do. It was a time when unemployment was still high, though not quite as bad as it had been a few years earlier. It was still bad enough, as the unemployed men from Jarrow would demonstrate the following year when they marched on London. The few cars that drove along Bridge Street had to take more care than usual. A new 30 mile an hour speed limit had just been imposed on all built-up areas. Leslie Hore-Belisha, the Minister of Transport, said that policemen beating gongs would halt offenders, so it is not just modern government departments that have odd ideas.

Left: Unlike many town centres Walsall has kept part of the character of its heritage, retaining some of the older buildings and an airy and spacious feel to a number of streets. The area around The Bridge still has a spacious feel to it and the attractively pedestrianised parts around here make it a pleasant shopping environment. Even just a gentle stroll during a lunch hour is a relaxed exercise. Of course there is restricted access for the motor car, unlike the situation here in the 1960s. Seen from Bradford Street the picture is little different 40 years on. The bank building still dominates the corner and people throng past it in large numbers going about their daily business. One of the busiest spots in town and a favourite meeting place for friends to linger and chinwag for a while, The Bridge was built across Walsall Brook, also known as Walsall Water, a tributary of the Tame. Bradford Street takes its name from the Earls of Bradford who owned lands and property in the vicinity. Any thoughts of connections with the county of the white rose would be wrong as this Bradford is the one in Shropshire. The earldom was restored in 1815 and the current earl is still Lord of the Manor.

Below: What a busy scene on Park Street in 1963. It must have been a bright and sunny day if the awnings are any guide, pulled down above the pavement to protect goods in the shop window from fading or perishing. Mary Quant and Carnaby Street had not had any effect upon Walsall fashion from the look of the styles worn by these shoppers, but the day was not far away when miniskirts and kinky boots would grace the legs of the young women on our streets. Even young men would start washing their hair more frequently as they put their jars of Brylcreem firmly to the back of the bathroom cabinet. Some things do not alter. Despite the coming of boutiques, Woolworth's would carry on its cheap and cheerful business. There was a branch on every main shopping street in the country and, despite being American in origin, 'Woolies' had become an integral part of British life. The 'five and ten cent' company came to our shores before World War I and has outlasted all manner of fads and fancies. Sometimes the service could be frustrating as the company seemed to employ girls who always asked you, when bringing a purchase to the till, 'How much is it, love?' But that was part of the fun of shopping there.

Below: The Co-operative building in the upper part of Bridge Street, seen in the 1950s, is an imposing building. Walsall adopted the style of co-operative retailing that officially first saw the light of day in Toad Lane, Rochdale in 1844. By 1862 a group called the Walsall Co-operative had acquired 166 members, but the Walsall and District New Co-operative Society did not come into being until 1885. Trading began in Hatherton Street before moving to Stafford Street and by the turn of the century other branches had opened. As well as provisions, boots, shoes, drapery, clothing, coal and hardware were all on sale. During the first half of the 20th century the Co-op divvy was important in encouraging housewives' custom and the holders of the family purse strings enjoyed putting stamps into their coupon books in the sure knowledge that they could be cashed in at a later date. By the time of this photograph the society had 78 shops with a turnover of £5 million and welcomed its 100,000th member in 1954. Three years later the Central Premises were refurbished and continued to flourish so much so that a new three storey block was opened in 1966 on Lichfield Street. Following a merger with the Kidderminster Society in 1980 the company was renamed the West Midlands Co-operative Society.

Right: High Street was the original main thoroughfare leading down from Church Hill, from where St Matthew's looks down upon this scene in May 1964. It was along here that the most impressive buildings in the town could once be found. As the way winds down to Digbeth (the dyke path) it follows the route of a once raised footway across the boggy ground. Markets have been held here for eight centuries since the first mention of one in 1220, though its official permit was not granted until 1399, by which time Walsall had already become a thriving market town. Market Cross was erected in 1386 in the middle of the road close to the junction with Upper Rushall Street. Two annual events were also held, known as the Onion Fair and the Orange Fair. When this image of market day was captured High Street was heaving with a seething mass of humanity. The traders rubbed their hands with glee at the level of business to be done and called out to customers with a mix of humour and advertising designed to encourage purses to be opened at their stalls. There was money to be spent on a few luxuries as well as essentials because the nation's economy was in good shape, jobs were aplenty and we had left the austerity of the postwar years far behind.

Below: How dependent we had become on the motor car by the end of the 1960s. Double yellow lines everywhere tried to limit the congestion on Bridge Street, but many drivers took the chance to park up for a few minutes whilst they did a quick shop. This could have been a Saturday afternoon, if the crowded pavements are any guide. Town planners have left most of the buildings to their own devices and we can still identify within this image today. Alterations have been made to the roadway but, otherwise, the traditional feel has been retained. Perhaps the shops are nowhere near as busy because the focus has moved in recent times to the Old Square and Saddlers shopping centres. Some good old standbys never change. Look at the 'Beetle' parked across the street. Germany's people's car, the Volkswagen, has had that distinctive shape for as long

as we can remember. Whilst other manufacturers have tinkered with their models, at one time adding fins and large chromium plated bumpers and at another going in for the sweeping lines of the hatchback, the VW goes on forever. It is not a coincidence that one of this country's top selling cars has largely kept its particular style. The Mini is still going strong and is similarly instantly recognisable.

Bottom right: It is March 1965 and the view along High Street market was taken from St Matthew's Church. The cross belongs to the outdoor pulpit that was erected in 1922. The camera angle helps us to appreciate the gradient of this part of town, for it required a certain amount of huffing and puffing to get up the pull from Digbeth to the top of the market. As shoppers caught their breath in between looking for bargains they might have reflected on the news coming over their transistor radios during that month. Whilst the world was concerned with such weighty issues as civil rights marches in Alabama, a Russian going for a walk in space and President Johnson sending US Marines into Vietnam, Britain had just one talking point of importance. The nation was agog for news of Goldie. He was the golden eagle that had escaped from London Zoo. For a fortnight he hogged the headlines and at one stage drew a crowd of thousands to Regent's Park, clogging the roads like a Bank Holiday rather than a wintry Sunday. Goldie enjoyed his freedom, gradually regaining strength in wings that had not been used properly for five years. Every so often he came down from a tree to eat titbits proffered by his fans and park rangers glumly commented that he could keep going for ages by gobbling up the park's ducks. When Goldie was recaptured on 10 March the news overshadowed the murder trial of the Kray twins that had just got under way.

Making a living

The squeamish and all vegetarians should look away now. Here an employee is removing a hide in one of the early stages in a process necessary for production in the leather industry that served our town well for centuries and put us on the international map. Even our local soccer team is known far and wide as 'The Saddlers'. Where would Mark Cross Ltd on Warewell Street or D Powell and Sons on Long Street have been without the raw materials of their trade? How would workers at Sedgwick's in Pleck or Whitehouse Cox of Marsh Street have earned a crust but for the hides upon which to exercise their talents? Leather working and saddlery did not really come into their own until the mid 19th century. Saddle ironmongery, the making of brasses, bits and buckles, had been going on for a number of centuries before the leather industry began to develop. It grew even further with leather ancillaries for riders and travellers, expanding into the field of lighter goods such as purses and bags. During the two world wars, despite the use of canvas webbing, there was a great demand for leather materials for both equipment and use by personnel. Leather footballs made in Walsall have also been used in a number of FA Cup Finals, the only pity being that the Saddlers were not there to kick them.

This was the way the modern kitchen looked in 1961. This housewife was showing it off to men whose job it was to promote gas space heating.

The changeover from traditional coal fires to central heating, whether it be by radiator or warm air flow, was one of the revolutions of this decade. The environmentalists got their way in the 1950s when a succession of Clean Air Acts restricted homes and industry in the types of fuel they were allowed to burn. Gradually the smog laden skies cleared as coal was replaced by smokeless fuel. Even cleaner still was the use of electricity and gas as a source of heat. Some homes burned oil, but storage was a problem and when petroleum prices rocketed in the 1970s it became even less attractive. The woman in the photograph had enjoyed dramatic changes in her housewife's role during the 1950s. Monday's washday had once been a drudge of boiling in the dolly tub, mangling over a bucket and pegging out in changeable weather. Twin tubs and spin dryers made her life, not to mention her poor hands, so much easier. She dispensed with the cold larder and bought a fridge on the never never and invested in an electric sewing machine, consigning the old treadle to the attic. Now she had the chance of gas space heating and never need get on her hands and knees to rake the ashes out of the firegrate ever again.

A key to longevity

The Midlands have a proud history of small yet tenacious engineering companies: one such is Birchill Automotive Presswork Ltd.

The business was founded in the late 19th century by WJH Goodman. The firm began life at 37 Harrison Street, Bloxwich at the Reliance Works where the firm's 20 or so employees made locks and hardware, particularly specialist and replacement six and seven lever locks as well as 'triangle key' locks for buses and the Gas Board, known as 'budget locks'.

During the second world war essential war work was undertaken such as making tank locks and frames for battery boxes, for the first time girls were employed, getting paid three halfpence for piecework for counter-sinking the battery boxes.

Both the founder's sons Harry and Joe, as well as his daughter Vera would be involved in the business. Harry took over the firm in the 1930s after the founder had died. In the 1950s Vera briefly controlled the business until Harry's son John - JH Goodman - finally took over and Joe, a gifted oil painter who owned a canal boat called 'Goody Two Shoes', left to take over as manager at a firm in Wolverhampton.

Meanwhile the firm had remained at its first premises until 1947 at which time it was supplying replacement locks to be used in the refit of the Queen Mary. A move was now made to Willenhall Lane Bloxwich, to a new Reliance Works. In the following years other businesses were acquired including Ashtree Locks & Hardware.

The firm went on to produce locks for Dennis Fire Engines and carriage locks and heaters for the railways. Production of exhaust components began in the early 1960s.

In 1970 the firm's current site in Green Lane was set up to start power press production of exhaust components which would become the principle business, although at that time Birchill's also made chassis members for Reliant cars as well as introducing locks for aluminium double glazed windows.

Today Birchill Automotive supplies exhaust systems to customers all over the United Kingdom and exports to Belgium, the Netherlands, Sweden, Germany, Eire and Malta.

Top left: *Staff pictured outside the Green Lane premises in the 1970s.* ***Left:*** *The modern interior of Birchill Automotive Products Ltd.*

Flying Dutchman inspires entrepreneurial growth on the double

Elshout is not a terribly common family name in the Midlands. But though it may not be a common one, it is certainly a familiar one to many in the region, it being the surname of Dutchman, Pim Elshout, who has lived in England since the 1960s. Pim is a man whose enterprise has created hundreds of jobs in the area and whose story is as extraordinary as it is inspirational.

From plastics to electronics today's AAC Group of companies has been built up over the decades to become a major player in British industry. The story of that group centres around one man Pim Elshout though many others were involved in his rise and that of the group of businesses he would eventually become chairman of.

Since 1979 AAC Plastics of Walsall has excelled to become one of the UK's leading manufacturers of vacuum formed, injection moulded and fabricated plastic components.

With two purpose built modern factories centrally located in Beecham Close, Aldridge and Stoneyford Road, Sutton in Ashfield the company now has a combined production area of 60,000 sq ft and employs over 150 experienced personnel. The established client base includes numerous blue chip companies from the retail, automotive, pharmaceutical, lighting and invalidity markets.

Company policy - to exceed customer expectations - has been a key factor in the firm's success and remains the key component of future development which offers innovative

design, quality and service at a competitive price. But what of its founder?

Pim Elshout was born in Holland and educated at Rotterdam Grammar School followed by four years at the Rotterdam School of Economics. After three years with a Dutch bank he joined Phillips Electrical in Eindhoven, Holland working in sales and in the light technical side of the business. But the ways of fate are always unexpected.

No doubt the young Pim expected his life to continue in Holland not the English Midlands. What linked Pim to England was the fact that like thousands of others he had a pen pal in Britain. For most of us who have had pen pals the distant relationship almost inevitably peters out over the years but Pim decided to visit

Top left: *Pim Elshout in a picture he sent to his penpal Barbara Wragg.*
Above right: *The picture Barbara sent to Pim.*
Right: *The group of friends who wrote for English penpals.*

so. In 1969 Aldridge Air Control was founded by Pim operating from above a draper's shop in Aldridge. A few months later Pim was joined by Roy Sudlow and Bert Bartlam and the company quickly began to grow.

Six years later, in 1975, another company was formed: AAC Plastics Ltd concentrated on plastic ductwork and fabrications in plastic. AAC Plastics would eventually move to a new one acre site in Aldridge and employ 75 people manufacturing for the lighting, display and point of sale industries.

It was in 1981 that a third company, AAC Eurovent Ltd, was formed to handle specialised building services contracts and deodorisation problems (using activated carbon) for the sewerage industry, the Ministry of Defence and industries where odour problems existed. Robin Elshout B.Sc. C.Eng. MCIBSE is now their Managing Director.

For most people three companies might have been enough but in 1983 Orbik Electronics was formed. It

the English girl who wrote to him and married her.
After marrying his English pen friend they settled in Sutton Coldfield where Pim joined the Carrier Engineering Co Ltd, a large heating and ventilation company, as a site clerk. Two years later Pim was promoted to manager of a local depot, from where all the West Midlands contacts were handled, managing around 150 men.

was a joint venture between Pim Elshout and Philip Elwell who had been, until then, the Deputy Managing Director of Mackwell Electronics.

Pim however was ambitious and with two colleagues he started a company called Richard Groves Ltd armed with just £250 and a bag of tools. That company was sold to the How Group in 1967; Pim however found he could not settle within the How Group and decided to start another business of his own.

For two years Pim carried on working for the How Group but his ambition to own his own business was undimmed and he planned how to set up another firm as soon as he was able to do

Top left: *The Drapers' shop, above which Pim founded Alridge Air Controls.* **Above:** *André and Robin, Pim and Barbara's sons.* **Above right:** *A line-up of company cars in the 1970s.* **Right:** *An early mobile exhibition unit.*

Philip became Managing Director and Pim Chairman. As with many new companies with hard work and enthusiasm and not a few lucky breaks Philip eventually achieved the turnover necessary to increase the administrative and works personnel; and he was fortunate in finding a young BSc qualified engineer, Ian Taylor, to help him with upgrading of existing designs and the product development which would take the company through the next five years.

The first 10 months, and £90,000 turnover, was carried out in an area no larger than a garage. More suitable rented premises were soon found in Middlemore Lane, Aldridge and it was here that Orbik consolidated the business achievements of its early days and welcomed new clients, tempted by the company's innovation, flexibility and competitiveness. By 1986 production and quality control levels were of a high enough standard to realise the target of doubling the turnover and by the end of the third year turnover had reached £600,000. Between 1986 and 1988 the company increased its customer base from 15 to 50 by which time turnover had reached £1.5 million. Building work on new premises just around the corner in Northgate were soon underway providing a 35,000 sq ft site with a massive expansion of the Laboratory and Quality Control Departments.

Orbik, established primarily to manufacture and sell emergency lighting, soon branched out into passive infra-red detectors and transformers. The company which started life in two rented rooms now moved into a wholly owned one acre site with purpose built offices, and a factory, employing some 70 people.

By 1990 Orbik Electronics had become the largest independent manufacturer of emergency lighting gear in the country. It was also

Top left: *Robin Elshout, Managing Director of AAC Eurovent Ltd.* **Above right:** *Barbara and Pim.*
Right: *André with one of the firm's fleet of service and delivery vans.*

producing electric and conventional transformers and printed circuit boards and had attained the coveted British Standard award BS 5750.

An in-house laboratory service and a customer service department at Orbik were by then able to provide customers with instant technical support, product design and development plus substantial analysis and testing resources. The company was now exporting to Hong Kong, Australia, Cyprus, Greece, Germany, Denmark and Sweden

By now Pim Elshout should have been thinking of retiring as he passed his 65th birthday. But retirement was still far off. And if retirement could not be celebrated then surely a birthday could? Pim was still fit enough to play five a side soccer at Wyndley leisure

units for the retail industry, Sainsbury's delicatessen counters, Somerfield, Kwik-Save and Tescos to display sweets and magazines in addition to work for Cadbury and Trebor Bassett.

By the opening years of the new millennium the AAC Group included not only AAC Plastics and Orbik Electronics but also manufacturing units such as the metal fabricators MetalForms.

The AAC story and that of its founder Pim Elshout is a truly remarkable tale and one which has inspired, and will continue to inspire other, now younger entrepreneurs. But how many young men from Walsall today we wonder would dare, or be able to do, as he did; how many of our young men here in Walsall could visit a pen pal in Holland and build up a group of businesses? Not many we'd bet. In the meantime Holland's loss has surely been our gain.

centre giving staff the idea of asking football legend and 1966 World Cup hero Gordon Banks to call at AAC plastics to present Pim with a silver rose bowl from the staff to commemorate this important date in 1991.

Sixty-five or not Pim was still full of energy and still pushing the Group forward. To complement AAC Plastic's vacuum forming facility, the AAC Group formed an injection moulding company to offer an additional service to new clients. Elsewhere all development and financing for the entire group of companies would be handled by AAC Group Services, an umbrella company providing corporate counselling, finance and specialised services.

Meanwhile a second generation of the Elshout family was making its presence felt. After starting in the business making number plates André Elshout became Managing Director of AAC Plastics with Pim Elshout as chairman. They were joined by current directors Ray Freeth and John Millard. By now the company was making display

Top left: *Pim, Philip Elwell, Teresa Adinall and Andrew Burman outside Orbik Electronics Ltd in 1990.*
Above left: *Pim with his hero, Gordon Banks, on his 65th birthday.*
Right: *André, now managing director of AAC Plastics.*
Below: *Company premises at Aldridge.*

Moulding the future

So where was your Millennium Falcon built? Not in a space-shipyard in 'A Galaxy Far Far Away' as a Star Wars fans might imagine but more prosaically in a plastics factory in the West Midlands.

Aldridge Plastics or simply 'the Plastics' has been a major employer in Aldridge for many years. In the 1970s the company was well known for the part it played in the manufacture of Action Man and his accessories followed by the Hungry Hippo game and later the Star Wars toys.

The company was incorporated in October 1968 as Park Lane Plastics (Aldridge) Ltd. Production commenced on Monday 3rd February 1969 with 28 employees. Four of the original employees would still be with the company more than 30 years later by which time 185 people would be on the payroll of what had become a multi-million pound business. That first morning however the auspices were not so good with staff greeted by six inches of snow.

Today the company's manufacturing facilities are equipped with the very latest Colortronic and vacuum delivery systems. The fully automatic press lines deliver mouldings untouched by human hand to quality control points and

Right: A view of the factory in the 1970s.
Below: An Aldridge Plastics exhibition stand, 1978.

huge investment programme assures customers of High Quality/Low Cost components.

Park Lane Plastics changed its name to Aldridge Plastics on 16th November 1971. The name Aldridge Plastics Ltd was not available in 1968, that name being still held by the General Electric Company (GEC) which had acquired the business name following its merger with Associated Electrical Ltd (AEI) in the mid 1960s.

Directors and senior executives from a Birmingham plastics company which relocated to London had founded the original Aldridge Plastics in 1954.

That earlier Aldridge Plastics was located in Middlemore Lane West on the Redhouse Industrial Estate, Aldridge. In 1957 the company joined the Siemans-Edison Swan group and became part of Associated Electrical Industries, it was then renamed AEI Plastics (Aldridge) Ltd. Subsequently following the AEI/GEC merger the company was closed down in early 1969 and its activities moved to the GEC site in Witton, Birmingham.

Park Lane Plastics (Aldridge) Ltd, which would become today's Aldridge Plastics, was founded by Albert Curtis, George Humpage, Eric Nicholls and David Breese. Up until then Albert Curtis had been Works Director for AEI Plastics (Aldridge) Ltd whilst his colleagues were engineers in the same company.

Two generations would come to be involved in the firm: wives and in-laws were involved from the outset alongside friends and acquaintances who helped out, whilst sons, daughters and a nephew of the founders would make their contributions felt too in due course.

In 1969 the new business opened at Unit 3 Morford Road, Northgate, Aldridge - premises which are still occupied - and began plastic injection moulding and assembly, mainly on sub contracting work for GEC and Lucas Electrical.

Albert Curtis became the first Managing Director; George Humpage and Eric Nicholls looked after the technical estimating and tool design. David Breese provided the expertise on the shop floor ensuring that the moulding machines ran properly; and in those early days everyone shared loading and unloading lorries and making the tea.

The firm's first injection moulding machine was bought second hand from GEC; it was an 8oz side-frame PECO plunger machine. The company also purchased two new 1oz Arburg Allrounder injection moulding machines followed by two new 3oz Bipel machines from BIP engineering Ltd in Streetly. For the technically minded the latter machines were equipped with screw plasticising units as compared to older plunger type equipment.

Inevitably many difficulties were encountered along the way before success could be assured: external forces such as the years of industrial unrest created the greatest difficulties with the miners, postal workers strikes, the three day week and the fuel crisis making their unwelcome contribution whilst decimalisation and years of high inflation also caused their own problems.

Competition from Japanese companies locating in the UK following Japanese investment and Government incentives did not help either, nor did competition from cheaper

Top: *An exterior view of the factory in the 1970s.*
Above: *A cartoon postcard commemorating the firm's opening.*

markets especially the Far East and later Eastern Europe. The collapse of the UK toy manufacturing industry would lead to nearly all such manufacturing going to the Far East. A spate of receiverships and liquidation's in the 1980s created many problems, the major one effecting Aldridge Plastics being one of its major customers Servis Domestic Appliances.

But despite these difficulties Aldridge Plastics continued to forge ahead, overcoming each obstacle as it arose and continuously expanding its production capacity. Apart from a short-lived incursion into a property in Lichfield in

the 1980s, and also leasing a small unit in Empire Close Aldridge for a few years, the company has remained at Morford Road taking up various small units as they became available until by 1980 a total of 20,000 sq ft was being occupied. Ultimately a large double unit on the opposite side of Morford Road was bought in the late 1980s adding a further 28,000 sq ft of manufacturing

space. By the mid 1990s, from its modest beginnings, Aldridge Plastics had achieved an annual turnover of almost £5 million.

Today Aldridge Plastics' main customers are makers of well known brands of domestic appliance and white goods, manufacturers such as Hotpoint, Creda, Hoover Panasonic and Intier Automotive seating. The company's vast knowledge acquired over many years in thermoplastic technology and processing has ensured continuing demand for its products. That professional competence is combined with a willingness to invest in plant offering state of the art technology: for example the Sandretto 500 tonne machine bought in 2002, whilst the eight moulding cells the firm would buy in the preceding 12 months would cost no less than £1 million.

Though machines may have changed completely many of the raw materials - polythene, polypropylene, polystyrene, Nylon and Acrylic - have remained largely the same. But although these basic polymers would still be used there would also be great advances in improving the physical and processing properties of the materials. Some new polymers would be introduced, mainly in the metal replacement fields and high temperature applications. Other polymers would be modified or filled with other substances such as talc, chalk, glass and carbon fibres along with many other materials to give improved

Top right: *Another Aldridge Plastics exhibition stand.*
Left: *Company founder, Albert Curtis with one of the famous Action Man bodies manufactured by the firm.*

performance in engineering applications such as weight and energy saving, food and medical applications and flame resistance.

Though the firm may have started off in what now seems like the steam age at a time when Star Wars and its

robots was entirely the stuff of fiction that fantasy future has become reality with robotic equipment installed in the latest moulding machines enabling very soft polymers to be removed without the use of ejector pins which might damage the components. Elsewhere the firm offers a range of operations which can be applied to products after the moulding process: silk screen printing, hot foiling, welding, spray painting and insert staking to provide an extraordinary product range from shirt buttons to large facia panels and trim for domestic washing machines. The company produces components weighing from 28 gm to 2,250 gm on a range of 36 injection moulding machines from 20 tonne clamp to 750 tonne clamp.

By the opening years of the new millennium founders Albert Curtis and George Humpage would both be retired though Eric Nicholls and David Breese would still be working as directors and looking to the firm's future, a future in which the company aims to expand into even more premises to enable development of more decorating facilities and diversification into assemblies and other activities utilising injection mouldings.

Despite its many growing pains the future of the company and the plastics industry now seems assured. Since the 1960s plastic has become an increasingly familiar part of everyone's daily lives. Plastic has replaced wood and metal in thousands of different applications over the last forty or more years - in toys, cars, domestic appliances and throughout industry.

Plastic's versatility is such that new uses are continually coming to the fore. We had the bronze age and the iron age and, in the 19th century, the steam age. The 20th century in turn saw the dawn of the age of plastic - an age which, despite some early scepticism has proved in the end to be an enduring one. With a combination of innovation and hard work the founders of Aldridge Plastics Ltd have ensured that the West Midlands has a place at the very heart of our modern age.

Top left: *A view of the 21st century factory.*
Left: *Company Directors proudly receive the Investors in People Award in 2000.*

Taking the lead

How long is it since man first domesticated the dog? Who can say? Man's best friend has been part of his life since before recorded history. Even the oldest of records from the Middle East, including the Bible, mention dogs. And cats too have been domesticated since the time of the ancient Egyptians.

No doubt the very first 'dog' to join man around his campfires was a deserted wolf cub who by his devotion and loyalty earned his place in accompanying man for the rest of history. Poor and rich alike came to value their pets. The only difference being that whilst the poor might make do and mend when it came to collars and leads the animals of the wealthy could be dressed as richly as their owners. Even today the very wealthy sometimes outfit their dogs and cats with golden collars studded with diamonds.

There is not much call for diamond encrusted dog collars in Walsall; but then jewels and precious metals are not necessary to make the best. For hundreds of years Walsall has been the home of the British leather

industry. One family business formed more than thirty years ago to specialise in producing dog collars and leads is still taking that local tradition forward; it has become one of the world's leading manufacturers offering discerning clients high quality products for pets.

Ancol Pet Products Ltd was established in August 1971 by Colin Lane to manufacture leather dog equipment. Colin had previously been the General Manager of a fancy leather factory and he named the new business after himself and his wife Ann. The firm's first premises, at 27 Lower Forster Street in Walsall were tiny - just 2,000 square feet - and they lacked parking facilities which made even receiving deliveries and sending out orders difficult.

The following year, 1972, was the year the firm received its first export order, an event which proved to be a major part of the firm's activities. Soon sales soared; collars, leads, muzzles and

Above: *Colin and Ann Lane exhibiting their products.*
Below: *The firm's premises pictured in 1975.*

harnesses began to be sold by the thousands. Ancol had tapped into a surprisingly buoyant market. By 1974 annual turnover was running at more than double the rate of the first year's trading. The labour force too had increased tenfold and the order book was still growing. To increase production capacity in the existing premises would have been at the expense of warehousing and despatch departments which themselves were by now too small. In September 1974 the fledgling firm moved into new larger premises in Leamore Lane Bloxwich, - Ancol House - which provided a production area six times larger than before and a similar increase in the size of warehousing and despatch departments.

Britons are famed for loving their pet dogs and cats. Perhaps that was why Ancol products would prove so popular. Those of us who own dogs like to reward their devotion by buying them collars and leads of the best quality we can afford, after all one can hardly give a dog a new hat for its birthday or a fountain pen for Christmas. Perhaps too the average dog owner has memories of the days when they could not afford to buy the best; perhaps they recall happy childhood days spent with the family pet playing in fields or bomb sites, chasing balls or throwing sticks in woods and

fields. Anyone who has ever owned a dog in childhood remains a 'doggy' person their whole lives. And even if, perhaps especially if, their childhood companion had to make do with a piece of rope instead of a proper leather collar and first class lead when in adulthood they do get the chance they invariably want to see that the devoted canine of today has the kind of 'clothes' which their predecessors could not have dreamed of.

Despite increasing sales of existing products new ones were constantly being developed by Ancol. The latter part of 1975 for example saw the marketing of a flea collar for cats which was an astonishing success. Sales showed another massive increase in demand.

Very soon space was again a major problem and alterations were made to the factory layout to increase production capacity. But by the end of 1976 there was no more room to bring in more labour and equipment.

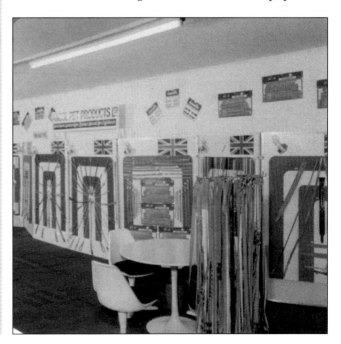

*Top left and right: Manufacturing the firm's products in the early 1970s. **Above left:** An advert for Ancol's pet collars and leads circa 1982.*
***Right:** Exhibiting Ancol's products in 1972.*

Sales by now were running at four times higher than they had been in 1974 and the labour force had trebled; and the order book was still growing.

At the beginning of 1977 Ancol acquired an additional factory in Leamore Lane, Bloxwich enabling the production area to be more than doubled. That year exports would amount to 60 per cent of the firm's output.

In 1984 Ancol moved its production yet again, this time to a 35,000 square foot site previously occupied by an engineering company, which offered premises all on one level, plus two acres of land capable of further development. Subsequently the company extended the premises to 50,000 square feet.

Ten years later the company could boast an annual turnover of four million pounds with half its sales being for export. That export sales should be so large may be something of a surprise to those who believe that foreigners don't have the same kind of affinity for their pets as the British. Certainly there are different attitudes to pets overseas but the extraordinary demand for Ancol's products suggests a rather different picture. The reputation of Britons as pet lovers combined with the British reputation for producing high quality craftsman made products undoubtedly combines in the minds of those who live around the world to create an irresistible combination in the minds of those foreigners who are devoted to their animals. 'If its good enough for British dogs and cats, it must be the best in the world' is the understandable and indeed accurate thought process which must go through the minds of dog and cat owners in every part of the globe.

The company's motto is 'quality, value and service'. To that can be added superb packaging and presentation with great attention paid to detail. Raw material for collars and leads is carefully selected English bridle

Top: *The factory floor in the 1990s.*
Above right: *One of Ancol's fleet of delivery vehicles.*

course synonymous with non-stick pans. But in 1994 it moved from pots and pans to products for pets. Ancol acquired the world exclusive rights to use Teflon on pet products. Teflon would be applied to leather during the tanning and finishing processes to form an invisible protection around each fibre making the leather much more resistant to oil and water based stains.

Teflon, a material undetectable by sight, smell or touch does not affect the natural suppleness or pliability of leather but simply strengthens it. The new Teflon coated range would be produced in three top selling colours Black, Mulberry and Forest green with brassed 'furnishings'. The resultant Timberwolf brand would be a decidedly up market product with a value for money image.

For dogs and cats time marches far faster than for humans. Though only one generation of humans yet measures the time since Ancol came into existence many generations of lucky pets have had the chance to be equipped with fine products from the Ancol range. Owners naturally feel proud to see their much loved pets wearing the best that money can buy, but who, on seeing a fine looking dog, or even more so a self satisfied looking cat, can doubt that being dressed with the best by their owners is not also a matter of intense pride for them too?

leather which is both strong and supple. Only the most experienced and skilled cutters trim the leather ready for stitching and finishing.

Meanwhile metal parts, 'furnishings', which at one time were all made in Walsall now come from the Far East and the traditional Walsall Hook has been replaced by the trigger hook.

Output is 75 per cent leather and 25 per cent nylon and rope products. Ancol also leads the market in pet combs produced from the finest materials and hand finished by skilled operators.

Cat collars come in a great variety from velvet, tartan and studded and the 'All Night Patrol' reflective safety collar. Production of cat collars reaching 50,000 each week made by 100 staff plus a team of outworkers, many previous employees with Ancol collecting and delivering their work.

Perhaps most surprising of product components is Teflon. Introduced by Du Pont in 1938 Teflon is of

Top left: *Loading finished products for distribution.*
Above left: *Colin Lane with his son, Simon.*
Below: *Exhibiting the firm's pet accessories in 2000.*

The 'power' behind traditional saddle making in Walsall

Many riders throughout the world have their own favourite saddle or bridle, for various reasons. They in some cases know they are made in Walsall, England, and some may think they are made in other European countries due to the exclusive names. The fact is they are very likely to have been made by one particular manufacturer in Walsall and have been since 1947.

For more than half a century, and for three generations of one family, Modern Saddlery (Walsall) and its associate company Gabriel Power & Co have been manufacturing saddles and bridle equipment, and in doing so have built up a world wide reputation for quality products.

Today the firm still produces top quality saddles and equipment made in the traditional manner. But sadly you won't see the Power name on any saddles or bridles for sale. The company specialises in 'Private Labels' - the practice of applying a customer's name or brand name to either flap and/or the 'head nails'. Or in some cases the customers have customised metal nameplates showing their own company name or logo tacked under the 'skirt'. What readers can be sure of however is that wherever and whenever they may have been looking at top quality saddlery the chances are that these skillfully hand made products have been manufactured in Walsall by the renowned Power family.

The roots of the Power family lie in Waterford, Eire where in the mid 19th century the Powers

Left: Company founder, Gabriel Power. Right: Valerie Power. Below: Saddle making in the early 20th century at Modern Saddlery.

were large land owners that incorporated many traditional businesses, one of these was glove and belt making. Gabriel Power's grandfather however left Ireland and became a glove maker in Birmingham. Gabriel Power was born in 1908 and later became a saddle maker.

War interrupted Gabriel's career; he joined the navy soon after the outbreak of the second world war and served in no fewer than 23 ships. He became a petty officer while serving aboard motor torpedo boats, then in 1946 left the navy and returned to saddlery.

Soon afterwards Gabriel went into partnership with Mr James Morris who had recently left the army and now worked as a saddler in Walsall. The new firm started out from premises in Bradford Street in 1947. The business became a limited company in 1950 when Mr James Morris sold his interest in the firm to Gabriel, but stayed on as saddle foreman until the 1980s. The company was then known as Modern Saddlery Walsall, modern by 1950s standard.

Gabriel then combined a bridle manufacturer he owned in Shaw Street with Modern Saddlery in Bradford Street. Then in 1959, in order to cope with the increasing volume of international orders the company was now receiving, he moved them both to a factory in Margaret Street. Helping to build up the business were members of Gabriel's family: his son John Power as well as his daughter Valerie, a saddle and bridle machinist who took charge of the hand stitchers and machinists at the factory. Gabriel Power died in 1965 a year before his new factory in Leamore Lane, Bloxwich (still the firm's home) was complete and his son John Power became managing director. The factory employed over 80 people and was an international success producing the first close contact jumping saddles in England. The 'Nelson Pessoa' saddle, named after the famous Brazilian show-jumper, and distributed through BWF in France, was first manufactured here and became the best selling jumping saddle in the world.

John Power also built up the business in the USA in the 1970s travelling widely from coast to coast finding new customers for his saddles and bridle goods, and attended trade shows in Philadelphia twice a year, to answer any technical questions they had. Over 20 wholesalers now stock his goods, to them the fact that they know the saddles and bridles are hand crafted from start to finish by experienced craftsmen using only the finest materials is the reason why they put their names and more importantly their reputations on these saddles. The same reputation then carried him forward in both Europe and the rest of the equine world.

When John Power died in 2001, 13 years after his sister, such was his stature and reputation as a true gentleman in business combined with his firm's reputation for quality, many of his American and European contacts flew to England to be at his funeral, both as friends and businessmen.

His son, Anthony Power, who started in 1987, learnt saddle making in all of its many disciplines from the foreman Mr Brian Bradbury, a well respected saddler who had served his apprenticeship under Gabriel Power. Anthony had travelled abroad with his father since 1998 and is currently taking the two companies of Gabriel Power & Co and Modern Saddlery forward using the self same traditional methods of manufacture and business ethics that his father taught him, something he is very proud to do.

Top left: John Power Exhibiting the firm's fine bridles in 1988, in Philadelphia, USA. Above right: John Power enjoying his products in Oregon, USA, in 1978. Below: Saddle making in the late 20th century at Modern Saddlery.

The staff of life

Bread - the staff of life, a truly natural food. Where would we be without it to make sandwiches, to mop up our gravy or to make our breakfast toast? Bread has been known for thousands of years, baked by housewives, (or perhaps that should be cave-wives) since time immemorial. So important is the idea of bread and home that even the very word 'man' is ultimately derived from one of our ancient words for loaf.

Did you know that Walsall's Harvestime Bakeries is the nation's largest producer of organic bread? Harvestime produced the first ever organic crusty sliced loaf; totally free from genetically modified ingredients - bread as nature intended.

How many husbands coming home from the fields and forests ravenous with hunger salivated as they sniffed the air as they detected the welcoming scent of newly baked bread waiting for them on their return.

No doubt thanks and appreciation were profuse; but that did not take the hard work out of the process. What housewives really needed was someone else to do the job for them. That demand and the emergence of cities in the Near East led eventually to specialisation and the arrival of the professional baker. Fresh bread daily was the watchword of those early bakers, just as it is today. Bakers even then worked through the night baking bread so that it would be ready for sale first thing each morning. And, for those who still preferred their own recipes but could not be bothered to light a fire in order to do the baking themselves, bakers offered another service - bring your own dough and we'll bake your bread for you! Such a service persisted down the centuries and was still common in England until relatively recent times: and in some cases it was a

Primitive ways of making bread can still be seen today in less developed parts of the world, with unleavened dough baked on flat heated stones. Who first learned to add yeast to dough in order to allow fermentation to take place and let the dough rise before baking is beyond recorded history - but the process was already well established in Mesopotamia and around the Mediterranean in classical times.

For housewives making bread has always been a hard if worthwhile task.

Above left: *Company founder, William Price.*
Right: *Price's Bread delivery carts from the early 1900s, taking part in a parade.*

soil. Today the company's organic bread is not only free from GM ingredients but is produced to Soil Association standards which means that it offers both purity and nutritional value suitable for vegetarian, vegan, and halal diets whilst being 97 per cent fat free.

Harvestime was founded in 1879 and has been baking quality bread ever since.

The company was begun by Birmingham born William Price at the tender age of just 16 years. William Price's business achieved rapid growth based on a formula of excellent products, innovation and by offering a better service than anyone else. The bread was originally, if unimaginatively, called 'Price's Bread' and sold with the slogan 'Price's Bread has spread because it's the best bread to spread'. Helped by his brothers and later their sons the business would become Britain's largest chain of bakers, and that by a handsome margin. By 1914, now known as 'Price Brothers', the firm would operate from over 200 locations in every town and city in the UK all owned by members of the Price family.

Between the wars the business was divided into five separate companies owned by different sections of the family. William Price and his four sons retained control of the Midland's business which also had bakeries in East Anglia and Liverpool; in the early 1920s this was

From Wheat Field To Consumer

We Mill the Flour and Bake the Bread and Specialise in Both

William Price & Sons Ltd.

wise precaution since - the adulteration of flour by any number of cheap substitutes such as chalk, straw, and dust by some unscrupulous bakers persisted far into the 19th century.

In Britain small corner shop bakers remained the dominant force in bread making until the second world war, but major changes in production capacity meant they would be progressively challenged by larger commercial bakeries operating on an industrial scale. One firm which would keep pace with those changing trends would be Walsall's Harvestime Bakeries.

The company began baking bread more than a century ago using only natural ingredients. Harvestime would go on to become one of the first large scale bread producers in Britain and to be one of the first to recognise the potential health benefits of organic foods. The company would demonstrate its responsiveness to modern concerns by developing a range of bread that is kind to the environment and to the

Top left: *An early delivery vehicle.* ***Above left:*** *An early poster advertising Price's bread.* ***Right:*** *A Harvestime delivery van from the mid 20th century.*

known as The Daily Bread Company though this was changed to William Price & Sons Ltd in 1926.

During the Depression of the late 1920s and 1930s and the tough war years beyond bread would fortunately continue to form the basis of the British diet. The vigorous Midlands branch of the business which came to Walsall in the 1930s thrived in spite of contracting demand and the predatory activities of major milling companies and North American bakers.

Most of the Price bakeries however were sold during the late 1930s and early 1940s which left operations polarised around the one site in Raleigh Street, Walsall.

Keeping the firm fit, lean and flexible enough to take advantage of changes in the industry and its market place remained a cornerstone of company policy, coupled with the confidence to make major invest-

ments in modern plant and technology. Many things changed after the second world war including eating habits and trade agreements and there were also considerable changes in technology. The company continuously adapted to meet the challenges posed by post-war Britain.

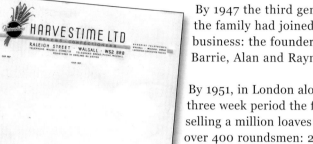

By 1947 the third generation of the family had joined the business: the founder's grandsons Barrie, Alan and Raymond.

By 1951, in London alone, over a three week period the firm was selling a million loaves delivered by over 400 roundsmen: 226 going round in electric vehicles, a mere 46 using petrol vans and 173 still horse drawn. There were no horses left however when in 1973 Harvestime Ltd was inaugurated as the operating subsidiary of William Price and Sons.

By the 1980s the company had completed a major investment

Top left: An early advertisement for Harvestime sliced bread. *Above:* An early Harvestime letterhead. *Below:* State-of-the art breadmaking facilities.

would include Lancashire, West Yorkshire, London, Wales and the South West. The Walsall and Leicester bakeries, strategically sited off the national motorway network, plus a distribution depot in Devon, would allow Harvestime to offer supplies of bread and morning goods to two thirds of England and Wales. Harvestime would produce a wide range of wrapped and crusty bread including white, brown, and wholemeal breads, rolls and 'morning goods' such as muffins and tea cakes found in many of the big supermarkets under the stores' own labels as well as being sold under the Harvestime brand name.

New product development has been central to the company which in recent years has established one of the largest crusty bread facilities in Britain with a range of over 50 breads in every variety shape and size. The firm also became the market leader in 'Instore Bakeries' with a 56 per cent share, whilst becoming the UK's largest producer of organic breads.

After more than 120 years in business Harvestime remains rightly proud of its top quality products combined with a totally reliable distribution service and the flexibility to respond rapidly to changing customer demands.

Top left: *Demonstrating some of Harvestime's range of products in one loaf.* ***Left:*** *Advertising Harvestime's range of Organic bread.* ***Below:*** *Brian Belleini, Company Secretary, left, Jonathan Price, Group Chief Executive, centre and Martin Price, Property Director, right, pictured in the late 1980s.*

programme in bakery plant, equipment and building expansion at Raleigh Street. The result was a trebling of production capacity and an increase in turnover from £4 million in 1979 to £20 million; by the end of the 1990s that turnover had reached £60 million.

The acquisition of a purpose built 200,000 sq ft bakery in Leicester in 1996 allowed Harvestime to maintain its growth and achieve an 8 per cent share in the £3 billion UK bread market.

Harvestime remains a growing, professionally managed private business. Now with bases in Leicester, north London, Maidstone and Cheshire in addition to Walsall it remains the main asset of the founding family whose fourth generation has now entered the business - the family now being represented by Alan's daughter Sue, Raymond's son Martin and Barrie's sons, Jonathan and Robin.

At the beginning of the new millennium Harvestime, by now with a thousand employees, would operate from two large modern bakeries. The business would have a capacity to produce 3.2 million loaves each day and would deliver to a vast geographical area that now

At the forefront of innovation since the Victorian age

Since the days of the horse drawn carriage, the name Albert Jagger Limited has been associated with innovation, service and the highest quality products for vehicles of all types.

The firm was established in 1887 by Albert Jagger and was originally a manufacturer of carriage lamps and many types of products for horse-drawn vehicles. In 1902, the company moved to Centaur Works in Green Lane, Walsall and again in 2001 to its purpose built premses, still in Green Lane.

By the beginning of the 20th century the firm, describing itself as a coach ironmonger and lamp maker, was offering to supply its customers with an astonishing range of products for the coach building trade: hundreds, indeed thousands of fittings redolent of that Edwardian age - iron goods such as foot plates and seat screws, hinges and bolts, roller bars and brake springs for dog carts, gigs, landaus and traps.

In its early days the firm was perhaps best known for high quality carriage lamps of various kinds which were hand-made by skilled craftsmen. Even by the early 1960s the company still received requests for the old type of carriage fittings and lamps, but that era had long passed.

Albert Jagger passed away in 1927, but the firm remained in the ownership of the Jagger family until the end of the second world war. In 1946, it was sold to Commander Douglas R Cooper whose own children and grandchildren would ensure that the business remained a family firm.

In the early part of the 20th century the business had slowly turned to the motor vehicle trade and over the years it progressed on that basis, always selling its products at

Above: *Company founder, Albert Jagger.* ***Below:*** *The Centaur Works in 1960s.* ***Inset:*** *An aerial view of Walsall, with the Centaur Works left of centre.*

was acting only as the firm's administrative headquarters and distribution centre; in addition there was a local manufacturing centre and a new plastic extrusions factory in Bloxwich, two other branches in Heywood and Romsey, a printing company in Walsall and a factory in New Zealand.

In the opening decade of the 21st century the firm of Albert Jagger Ltd has seen the reign of five monarchs and during that time has evolved to meet the ever-changing needs of its clients. When Albert Jagger founded the firm in 1887 no-one could have predicted that the horse drawn carriage trade which he aimed to supply would come to an end. Many firms, failing to understand the motor car's inevitability, did not change to meet the new needs of the new century and disappeared for ever; a few, like Jaggers, rose to the challenge.

The leather, nickel, brass and malleable iron of the 19th century has now been replaced by the mild steel, stainless steel and plastics of the 21st century. The many hundreds of items now supplied by Jaggers however still take the breath away: detachable corner pillars, cargo straps and mounting brackets, spring-hooks, hinges, locks and handles, mudflaps and window fittings. With a reputation for being able to supply a part or fitting for anything on wheels, from a trailer to a tractor Albert Jagger Ltd has successfully maintained its reputation as a major force in the commercial vehicle and allied industries worldwide ever since the reign of Queen Victoria.

the keenest prices to become one of the largest suppliers of its kind in the United Kingdom.

The last craftsman of the carriage lamp age died in 1948 after having served the company for 60 years, though leaving a son and grandson still working for the firm. That length of service would be neither unique, nor the record, with one member of staff who joined the firm in 1888 remaining with the firm until 1951.

Innovation was the order of the day. In the late 1950s Jaggers acquired plastic moulding machines making its own moulds. The company recognised quite early that many vehicle fittings and accessories were especially suitable for mouldings in plastic and as opportunities arose more and more were redesigned and made from plastic.

By the late 1980s Albert Jagger Ltd had become the acknowledged leader in the manufacture and supply of parts and fittings to vehicle body builders in over 100 countries, with the half man half horse centaur trademark becoming synonymous with quality and innovation.

By then the Centaur Works, not used for manufacture since before the 1939-45 war,

Top left: *A more close-up bird's eye view of the Centaur Works in the 1970s.* **Above left:** *The firm's new premises in Green Lane.* **Below:** *A general aerial view of Walsall in 2000.*

At the cutting edge

Axes for all purposes, builders' and slaters' hammers and picks, garden tools, bill hooks and slashers, brushing hooks, agricultural implements and butchers cleavers. These items all have one thing in common: they are all cutting tools.

Anyone who regularly handles tools knows the difference that the right tool makes to the job. And if the right tool is also the best of its kind what may have seemed a hard job can become an easy one. All workmen value quality tools.

Deep in the heart of industrial England amidst the great Midland area of mines, factories and plants devoted to large scale mass production there is an industry still dependent upon native craftsmanship and individual technical experience to produce perfect hand tools.

With its trademark of a charging bull the undisputed star of that industry is Bullock Tools or, to give the business its Sunday-best name, the Bullock Brothers (Edge Tools) Ltd based at the Plant Edge Tool Works at Cheslyn Hay.

There is a wide range of Bullock tools of many different types designed to serve many purposes. Each tool is a precision instrument in its design, finish, fine balance and strength. Every Bullock tool is hand forged from the finest steel using decades of practical experience and patient research to ensure their consistent quality. They are made for hard work and a long life and to stand up to rough handling in any part of the world.

Above: *Pages from an old Bullock Brothers product brochure.*
Right: *An exhibition of Bullock tools in 1976.*

Though some designs are unique to Bullock Tools most represent the extraordinary range of tools demanded and developed, sometimes over centuries by a plethora of trades and activities from farming to mountaineering.

A glance through the Bullock catalogue is a revelation. How many kinds of axe can *you* name? Bullocks have made at least sixteen different kinds from the familiar household hatchet of our youth to the less familiar mountain climber's ice axe and no fewer than three different kinds of fireman's axe.

It is however the Bullocks agricultural range of implements which is most evocative of a rural life which many may have thought had disappeared completely, a world of farming which few could ever imagine could be so diverse in the deceptively simple hand tools it would use

Isn't a bill hook just a bill hook? Not at all; it seems that every part of Britain's rural community and further afield has its own favourites: the Yorkshire Bill, the Hampshire Bill, the Devon, the Wiltshire and the Sussex not forgetting other seven more mysteriously named such as the Ceylon Tanged Cattie, the

wholesalers across the United Kingdom.

Despite intense competition from cheap imports the undisputed quality of Bullock tools ensures their continuing popularity alongside the firm's ability to even make tools to individual customers' specifications

The pleasure of owning mass produced implements is invariably tarnished by the knowledge that we seldom get the best possible product. The best requires real craftsmanship which is seldom found in goods produced by the million. Discerning buyers want the best, and that can only be found by seeking out products made in traditional ways by real craftsmen.

With three generations of the Bullock family having been involved in the business, and with Brian Bullock now managing director and Robert Bullock the current company secretary, today Bullocks Tools is looking forward to seeing its superbly crafted products becoming even more popular in the new millennium.

Farrington Extra Wide and the Irish Slasher or the Heavy Sir Tatton Sykes Slasher. From sileage knives to butchers cleavers and garden shears to turfing irons Bullocks seems to have made them all!

Bullock Brothers pioneered the 'sold forged' principle and all its tools, whether slashers or 'langet' types, are made from a single piece of steel with no weld whatsoever which adds immeasurably to their efficiency and longevity.

Founded in 1952 by Albert George Bullock, a former engineering blacksmith, the firm began life at Great Wyrley where the founder's father, brother, and eventually his two sons, would work as edge tool manufacturers and drop forgers.

For more than half a century now Bullock tools have been exported around the world being especially popular in Eire, Germany, the USA and New Zealand as well as being found in builders suppliers and

Above, all three pictures: *Different processes in the manufacture of Bullock Brothers tools.* ***Below:*** *Bullock Brothers yard pictured in 1976.*

St Mary's Scouts parading along Lichfield Street in the 1950s.

Acknowledgments

The publishers would like to thank

Walsall Local History Centre -
part of the Leisure and Community Services department of Walsall MBC
Walsall Observer
Alan H Price
Jack Haddock
Cath Yates
Andrew Mitchell
Steve Ainsworth

True North Books Ltd - Book List

Memories of Accrington - 1 903204 05 4
Memories of Barnet - 1 903204 16 X
Memories of Barnsley - 1 900463 11 3
Golden Years of Barnsley -1 900463 87 3
Memories of Basingstoke - 1 903204 26 7
Memories of Bedford - 1 900463 83 0
More Memories of Bedford - 1 903204 33 X
Golden Years of Birmingham - 1 900463 04 0
Birmingham Memories - 1 903204 45 3
Memories of Blackburn - 1 900463 40 7
More Memories of Blackburn - 1 900463 96 2
Memories of Blackpool - 1 900463 21 0
Memories of Bolton - 1 900463 45 8
More Memories of Bolton - 1 900463 13 X
Bolton Memories - 1 903204 37 2
Memories of Bournemouth -1 900463 44 X
Memories of Bradford - 1 900463 00 8
More Memories of Bradford - 1 900463 16 4
More Memories of Bradford II - 1 900463 63 6
Bradford Memories - 1 903204 47 X
Bradford City Memories - 1 900463 57 1
Memories of Bristol - 1 900463 78 4
More Memories of Bristol - 1 903204 43 7
Memories of Bromley - 1 903204 21 6
Memories of Burnley - 1 900463 95 4
Golden Years of Burnley - 1 900463 67 9
Memories of Bury - 1 900463 90 3
Memories of Cambridge - 1 900463 88 1
Memories of Cardiff - 1 900463 14 8
Memories of Carlisle - 1 900463 38 5
Memories of Chelmsford - 1 903204 29 1
Memories of Cheltenham - 1 903204 17 8
Memories of Chester - 1 900463 46 6
More Memories of Chester -1 903204 02 X
Memories of Chesterfield -1 900463 61 X
More Memories of Chesterfield - 1 903204 28 3
Memories of Colchester - 1 900463 74 1
Nostalgic Coventry - 1 900463 58 X
Coventry Memories - 1 903204 38 0
Memories of Croydon - 1 900463 19 9
More Memories of Croydon - 1 903204 35 6
Golden Years of Darlington - 1 900463 72 5
Nostalgic Darlington - 1 900463 31 8
Darlington Memories - 1 903204 46 1
Memories of Derby - 1 900463 37 7
More Memories of Derby - 1 903204 20 8
Memories of Dewsbury & Batley - 1 900463 80 6
Memories of Doncaster - 1 900463 36 9
Nostalgic Dudley - 1 900463 03 2
Memories of Edinburgh - 1 900463 33 4
Memories of Enfield - 1 903204 14 3

Memories of Exeter - 1 900463 94 6
Memories of Glasgow - 1 900463 68 7
More Memories of Glasgow - 1 903204 44 5
Memories of Gloucester - 1 903204 04 6
Memories of Grimsby - 1 900463 97 0
More Memories of Grimsby - 1 903204 36 4
Memories of Guildford - 1 903204 22 4
Memories of Halifax - 1 900463 05 9
More Memories of Halifax - 1 900463 06 7
Golden Years of Halifax - 1 900463 62 8
Nostalgic Halifax - 1 903204 30 5
Memories of Harrogate - 1 903204 01 1
Memories of Hartlepool - 1 900463 42 3
Memories of High Wycombe - 1 900463 84 9
Memories of Huddersfield - 1 900463 15 6
More Memories of Huddersfield - 1 900463 26 1
Golden Years of Huddersfield - 1 900463 77 6
Nostalgic Huddersfield - 1 903204 19 4
Huddersfield Town FC - 1 900463 51 2
Memories of Hull - 1 900463 86 5
More Memories of Hull - 1 903204 06 2
Memories of Ipswich - 1 900463 09 1
More Memories of Ipswich - 1 903204 52 6
Memories of Keighley - 1 900463 01 6
Golden Years of Keighley - 1 900463 92 X
Memories of Kingston - 1 903204 24 0
Memories of Leeds - 1 900463 75 X
More Memories of Leeds - 1 900463 12 1
Golden Years of Leeds - 1 903204 07 0
Memories of Leicester - 1 900463 08 3
More Memories of Leicester - 1 903204 08 9
Memories of Leigh - 1 903204 27 5
Memories of Lincoln - 1 900463 43 1
Memories of Liverpool - 1 900463 07 5
More Memories of Liverpool - 1 903204 09 7
Liverpool Memories - 1 903204 53 4
Memories of Luton - 1 900463 93 8
Memories of Macclesfield - 1 900463 28 8
Memories of Manchester - 1 900463 27 X
More Memories of Manchester - 1 903204 03 8
Manchester Memories - 1 903204 54 2
Memories of Middlesbrough - 1 900463 56 3
More Memories of Middlesbrough - 1 903204 42 9
Memories of Newbury - 1 900463 79 2
Memories of Newcastle - 1 900463 81 4
More Memories of Newcastle - 1 903204 10 0
Memories of Newport - 1 900463 59 8
Memories of Northampton - 1 900463 48 2
More Memories of Northampton - 1 903204 34 8
Memories of Norwich - 1 900463 73 3
Memories of Nottingham - 1 900463 91 1

Continued overleaf

True North Books Ltd - Book List

More Memories of Nottingham - 1 903204 11 9
Bygone Oldham - 1 900463 25 3
Memories of Oldham - 1 900463 76 8
Memories of Oxford - 1 900463 54 7
Memories of Peterborough - 1 900463 98 9
Golden Years of Poole - 1 900463 69 5
Memories of Portsmouth - 1 900463 39 3
More Memories of Portsmouth - 1 903204 51 8
Nostalgic Preston - 1 900463 50 4
More Memories of Preston - 1 900463 17 2
Preston Memories - 1 903204 41 0
Memories of Reading - 1 900463 49 0
Memories of Rochdale - 1 900463 60 1
More Memories of Reading - 1 903204 39 9
More Memories of Rochdale - 1 900463 22 9
Memories of Romford - 1 903204 40 2
Memories of St Albans - 1 903204 23 2
Memories of St Helens - 1 900463 52 0
Memories of Sheffield - 1 900463 20 2
More Memories of Sheffield - 1 900463 32 6
Golden Years of Sheffield - 1 903204 13 5
Memories of Slough - 1 900 463 29 6
Golden Years of Solihull - 1 903204 55 0
Memories of Southampton - 1 900463 34 2
More Memories of Southampton - 1 903204 49 6
Memories of Stockport - 1 900463 55 5

More Memories of Stockport - 1 903204 18 6
Memories of Stockton - 1 900463 41 5
Memories of Stoke-on-Trent - 1 900463 47 4
More Memories of Stoke-on-Trent - 1 903204 12 7
Memories of Stourbridge - 1903204 31 3
Memories of Sunderland - 1 900463 71 7
More Memories of Sunderland - 1 903204 48 8
Memories of Swindon - 1 903204 00 3
Memories of Uxbridge - 1 900463 64 4
Memories of Wakefield - 1 900463 65 2
More Memories of Wakefield - 1 900463 89 X
Nostalgic Walsall - 1 900463 18 0
Golden Years of Walsall - 1 903204 56 9
More Memories of Warrington - 1 900463 02 4
Memories of Watford - 1 900463 24 5
Golden Years of West Bromwich - 1 900463 99 7
Memories of Wigan - 1 900463 85 7
Golden Years of Wigan - 1 900463 82 2
Nostalgic Wirral - 1 903204 15 1
Memories of Woking - 1 903204 32 1
Nostalgic Wolverhampton - 1 900463 53 9
Wolverhampton Memories - 1 903204 50 X
Memories of Worcester - 1 903204 25 9
Memories of Wrexham - 1 900463 23 7
Memories of York - 1 900463 66 0